Psychology in Action

PSYCHOLOGY IN ACTION

Psychology has a great deal to say about how we can make our working lives more effective and rewarding: the way we see other people, how they see us, and our ability to communicate with others and achieve what we want from a situation. Starting from actual practice in the classroom, the police station, the surgery or the interviewing room, PSYCHOLOGY IN ACTION looks at the everyday working methods and concerns of particular groups of people and asks: where and how can psychology help?

COUNSELLING
AND HELPING

Stephen Murgatroyd

Professor of Applied Psychology,
Athabasca University, Alberta, Canada

BPS
BOOKS

ROUTLEDGE

Published by The British Psychological Society
and Routledge

First published in 1985 by The British Psychological Society, St Andrews House, 48 Princess Road East, Leicester LE1 7DR, in association with Routledge Ltd, 11 New Fetter Lane, London EC4P 4EE.

Reprinted 1986, 1988, 1990, 1992, 1995, 1996

British Library Cataloguing in Publication Data

Murgatroyd, Stephen
Counselling and helping. — (Psychology in action)
1. Counselling
I. Title II. Series
361.3'23   BF637.C6

ISBN 0-901715-43-3
ISBN 0-901715-41-7 Pbk

Library of Congress Cataloging in Publication Data

Murgatroyd, Stephen J.
Counselling and helping.

Includes index.
1. Helping behavior.   2. Counseling.   I. Title.
BF637.H4M87   1986   158'.3   85-18742

ISBN 0-901715-43-3
ISBN 0-901715-41-7 Pbk

Set in Compugraphic Mallard
by AB Printers Limited, 33 Cannock Street, Leicester LE4 7HR
Printed and bound in Great Britain by Hobbs the Printers Ltd,
Brunel Road, Totton, Hampshire SO40 3WX

Dedication

This book is dedicated to Horace and Denise Murgatroyd (my parents), Marcel Leclerc (my grandfather), Michael and Ivy Apter, Richard and Gilly Gale, the Coping with Crisis Research Group at the Open University, and students and staff at University College, Cardiff, the Open University, the University of Saskatchewan and the Gabriel Dumont Institute in Ile-à-La-Cross.

CONTENTS

Introduction

This is not a comprehensive book about counselling and helping –
it is an introduction. It seeks to:

- examine the basic features of helping and counselling
relationships
- describe and explain a variety of helping and counselling
strategies appropriate across a number of helping relationships
- instruct readers in the tactics of helping and counselling
appropriate to each of the strategies
- examine the different settings in which these strategies can be
used.

The book is not an academic text, though it is based on an
approach to counselling and helping which can be fully supported
by available research. However, for those wishing to follow up the
more academic aspects, references are given at the end of most
chapters.

It is assumed that you are actively engaged in helping activities of
some kind or other, wish to examine ways of developing your skills
and expand your awareness of helping, and you will use this book
in a way appropriate to your needs. Finally, I hope you will adopt
and adapt the ideas and suggestions made here in a way that
matches your own way of working and your own situation.

This book is for social workers and their assistants, nurses and
doctors, lawyers, teachers, volunteer counsellors and helpers, suicide prevention workers, marriage guidance counsellors, career
workers and community development workers. Since the audience
is so broad it is difficult to provide examples and case materials
appropriate to each group. You will therefore need to convert the
ideas and principles to your own situation.

Some of the practical suggestions made here may be 'too risky' for you to undertake. If they strike you in this way do not undertake them. But do explore why you feel this way. Ask yourself, 'How can I find more ways of taking risks without putting at risk those I am trying to help?'

Counselling and helping are sometimes seen as separate activities. I see them as synonymous. So I do not use words like 'client' or 'patient' as descriptions of the person in need and I prefer the word 'helper' as a description of the work of a counsellor, social worker or therapist. I do not share the view of many counsellors and therapists who regard extensive professional training and certification as a prerequisite for the practice of some of the tactics described here. In all my previous writing I have attempted to demystify and deprofessionalize counselling, and this book is no exception. Counselling is a specialized form of improvised drama and most of the 'difficult' work described here is commonplace in drama improvisation workshops. What matters most is not the certification of helpers but their genuineness and their commitment.

I do not think there is a 'right' approach to helping and counselling. Each helper has to find an approach which is right for them. The materials presented here are intended to help you explore your own approach so that you can more accurately match your strategies and tactics to the needs of the person you are helping.

A book cannot substitute for experience; nor can it provide sufficient details for you to go out and use the complex and sometimes demanding skills it describes here. If you are just beginning to develop your skills as a counsellor, you are strongly advised to follow the suggestions made in Chapter 9 about supervision and support.

Counselling and helping are generally presented as serious endeavours, which, indeed, they are. They can also be amusing and fun. Though helpers need to be careful not to use humour cynically, humour has a clear place in helping. So too does enjoyment. Helpers often find themselves faced with distressing experiences; but sometimes such experiences turn into vitally important moments of personal development. These two features – enjoyment and development – are under-represented in this book, but not forgotten.

Comments about and reactions to this book are welcome. Please write to Stephen Murgatroyd, The Open University in Wales, 24 Cathedral Road, Cardiff CF1 9SA, Wales, U.K.

Part 1. Foundations

Chapter 1

Counselling as Helping

A great many people seek help from others. The mother of a young child will seek the help of friends or relatives when faced with the practical or emotional difficulties of being a parent. Someone at work may seek the help of a colleague when the job becomes stressful or when a critical decision has to be made. A couple may seek the help of a counsellor when their marriage begins to fail and divorce looks possible. An unemployed teenager may seek help and counsel others in an attempt to help them come to terms with their situation. A pupil at a secondary school may seek the help of a teacher or the school nurse or an aunt or uncle about their choice of subjects. Helping is a common feature of everyday life.

Helping and counselling are *not* professional activities – these words are descriptions of the attempts peple make to help others in some way. Consequently, nurses, doctors, dentists, receptionists, bar staff, teachers, social workers, and air stewardesses can all find themselves acting as helpers and counsellors to a person in need.

So common is helping as an activity that we often do not fully notice the attempts we make to help other people. Phrases such as '... if I were you ...' or ' ... now, when that happened to me ...' or '... have you thought of ...' have become commonplace in the vocabulary of friendship and acquaintance. Such phrases tell us that some form of helping is taking place.

Forms of helping

There are a variety of ways in which one person can provide help to others. Here are some brief illustrations of how one person can be helped by another:

- Sally was unsure whether she was entitled to maternity leave in the company for which she worked – a friend within the company explained to her the legal rights of women to maternity leave and the company policy. Sally was helped by being *given information*.

- Jack is very ill and unable to cook for himself. He lives alone and has few friends. Mary, his neighbour, cooks him a meal each day and makes sure that he has some groceries for a snack whenever he feels hungry. Jack is helped by Mary's *direct action*.

- Simon finds a particular encounter he has each month with his supervisor very stressful. So stressed is he before these meetings that he develops headaches and stomach upsets. This stress occurs despite the fact that the supervisor has nothing but praise for his work. Dennis shares with Simon some techniques for relaxation which help Simon control his stress and Simon soon stops experiencing the physical symptoms. Here Simon is helped by the *teaching and coaching* he receives from Dennis.

- A team of social workers has a high staff turnover during a particular period. What has happened is that the team has been given too large an area to cover and so has an excessive caseload. An outside consultant is brought in and helps this team present their case and secure a change in the distribution of responsibility within the social work department. This results in a reduction in caseloads. By *changing the system* individuals are helped directly.

- Sue, a nurse, feels that she is being victimized because she supported a walk-out by cleaning staff in the hospital. She feels that she is not being regarded as eligible for promotion because of her association with the striking cleaners. Her nursing officer takes up her case, acts as advocate on her behalf, and secures a place for her on a short-list for promotion. Sue is helped directly by this *advocacy* of her case.

- John feels that he is unable to make relationships with people and that few people show any appreciation of his work. One of his colleagues, Barry, starts to provide John with feedback on what his behaviour looks like and how something he has said is received by others. John seeks to learn from this feedback and uses it to try and improve his relationships with others in general and Barry in particular. As time passes, Barry provides increasingly confrontative feedback which makes John think carefully about how he might improve his social skills. Through *genuine feedback*, offered in a spirit of friendship, John is helped to change.

- Mike and Angie have been married for 12 years and they are starting to feel that their marriage is a little stale. Mike says that he is bored and Angie says that she feels like having fun and excitement, but is not sure that Mike is able to provide it. They seek help from a marriage guidance counsellor, who helps them identify their situation in more detail and encourages them to explore ways of changing it. This *counselling* significantly enhances the quality of their marital relationship.

These brief examples of helping and counselling introduce seven basic forms of helping – giving information, direct action, teaching and coaching, systems change, advocacy, providing feedback and counselling. You will notice that these different forms of helping are not described in terms of *who* it is that provides the help but rather in terms of *what the nature of helping is*. I cannot agree that only certain kinds of people (for example, professional counsellors with specified academic qualifications) should be allowed to provide particular forms of help. On the contrary, it is a central principle throughout this text that helping is a *process* that can be and is widely used and available within a community and it is not the sole prerogative of professionalized helpers and counsellors. Professional helpers and counsellors offer specialized services to some communities and groups, yet a great many areas are not served by professionals: help is given by individuals with little, if any, training, but with considerable experience and insight. It is to these 'lay' helpers that this book is primarily addressed.

The seven forms of helping briefly illustrated here imply that:

- helping can take place in a variety of settings and in a variety of circumstances
- helping can be concerned with an individual, a group, or with a kind of problem
- helping can involve the helper working at the level of an individual, a family, an organization or a community
- there are a variety of forms of helping (not one right and several wrong ways) and that providing help may involve using a variety of helping strategies.

Helpers therefore need to recognize that their work will involve choosing appropriate strategies and tactics to suit the circumstances in which they are working.

For my present purposes, helping is about enabling people to change. The change may be slight – helping someone understand – or it may be a major change in the way they think and feel about something. The aim of helping is to assist someone to take more control of their own life.

Counselling as helping

Defining helping in this way makes helping similar to many of the definitions of counselling offered in specialist books. For example, the American Psychological Association's Division of Counseling Psychology defines counselling as 'helping individuals towards overcoming obstacles to their personal growth, wherever these may be encountered, and towards the optimal development of their personal resources'. This is similar to the definition offered by Anne Jones, a leading British counsellor, who defines counselling as '... an enabling process, designed to help an individual come to terms with his or her life as it is and ultimately to grow to greater maturity through learning to take responsibility and to make decisions for him or herself'. Counselling can thus be regarded as a particular form of helping.

Yet counselling is often viewed as something that is a highly skilled and professional activity, requiring substantial training and a great deal of emotional maturity on the part of the counsellor. Psychological counselling *does* involve competences and skills and professional training. But such counselling is practised only rarely and by a select few. A great deal of counselling is practised by a variety of people who have developed their skills through experience, reading, and sharing their ideas and concerns with others. These are counsellors just as much as psychological counsellors. They offer an invaluable service.

The helping process

John Heron, a British counselling psychologist, suggests that there are six strategies for helping which are commonly used by those who work in intimate helping relationships. These are:

Prescriptive – giving advice, being judgemental: the helper seeks to direct the behaviour of the person in need, especially the behaviour that occurs outside the helping relationship.

Informative – being didactic, interpreting or giving instruction: the helper seeks to impart new information to the person in need, which is intended to shape their subsequent behaviour, thoughts or feelings.

Confronting – giving direct feedback, challenging: the helper uses a variety of techniques to challenge the restrictive attitudes, values, behaviours, thoughts and/or feelings of the person in need so as to help this person recognize and change these features in themselves.

Cathartic – encouraging emotional discharge: the helper uses facilitative techniques intended to enable the person in need to release and directly experience emotion (sadness, joy, tension, pain, sorrow, excitement, etc.) which has hitherto been kept 'locked' within them so that they may use the experience of release as a basis for better self-understanding and personal development.

Catalytic – being reflective, enabling self-direction: the helper encourages the person in need to take control of the programme of helping by directing the attention of the helper to their needs and by negotiating a helping contract in which rights, duties and tasks are clearly defined so that the skills of the helper can be used to enable the person to take greater control of their own life.

Supportive – being approving, consolidating, suggesting organizational structures: the helper seeks to assist the person in need to accept their own development and to develop mutual support structures.

These six general strategies can be grouped to form two major styles of helping. These are: (a) the *prescriptive or directive style* – where the helper directs, instructs or guides the person in need to an appropriate action; and (b) the *facilitative or developmental style* – where the helper is less directive and seeks to encourage the person in need to discharge emotion and to reach their own realizations of appropriate actions.

Let me illustrate these styles by reference to some case material:

Susan says she is very shy. She finds meeting new people very anxiety-provoking and avoids doing so whenever possible. Even when she knows people very well it is rare for her to speak and initiate conversation. Her friend encourages her to seek help with this problem from a counselling service. The counsellor provides an opportunity for Susan to rehearse some conversations with strangers. He provides some routines which she can use whenever she starts to feel anxious – routines which both reduce the stress and enable her to function in the social situation she finds herself in. He trains her to initiate certain kinds of conversations with strangers – in shops and cafés – and accompanies her on her attempts to use these techniques. Essentially, he trains her to develop social behaviours. Over a period of six months Susan becomes more confident and begins to have a more active social life – something she is very pleased about.

In contrast, another counsellor is working with Len, who has the same problem as Susan. Rather than offer Len a training programme, this counsellor encourages Len to explore the history of the problem in his life and to associate the problem with the way he feels about other people (especially his mother and father and his brother). On several occasions during counselling sessions Len gets very upset and the counsellor works with Len to identify these feelings he experiences and to give them meaning. Gradually, Len becomes more confident in disclosing to the counsellor more and more about himself. This increase in self-disclosure is accompanied by a greater willingness to talk to others. After five months, Len stops coming to the counsellor – he feels he is making enough progress on his own.

It is not difficult to identify the first strategy as directive and the second as facilitative. Notice, though, that both strategies produced results which those being helped felt happy with.

Different kinds of counselling and helping services in the community will use one or the other of these different strategies at different times. For example, lawyers and doctors often provide information which directs a person in need to a particular course of action and can be regarded as being generally more directive than facilitative. In contrast, marriage guidance counsellors and those workers who offer telephone counselling services for suicide callers, gays or students tend to be more facilitative than directive. Whilst these statements may be generally true as statements about the nature of an organization's helping style, particular members of these organizations may be more facilitative than directive and particular persons in need using the service of some helpng agency may need more directive than facilitative services. The point to note is that there are different strategies for helping, and an individual helper should be conscious of the particular strategy they use most frequently. In addition, helping agencies ought to be aware of the predominant strategy for helping used within that organization.

You should notice an important point here. It has not been suggested that one strategy is 'better than' or 'more common than' another. What has been said is that helpers need to be conscious of the strategy they use. They also need to be conscious of the effect their strategy has upon those they are seeking to help. Not all those who come to a 'directive' agency will prefer a directive strategy; in contrast, some of those who seek marriage guidance become frustrated with the less directive and more facilitative strategy and ask their counsellors for more direction. Effective helping involves the helper taking active steps to match their strategy for helping with the needs of the person in front of them. A failure to achieve this can lead to the premature ending of a helping relationship.

Another point worth making about the six strategies for helping described here is that helpers will find themselves moving between some or all of them both with different people and with the same person on different occasions. Helpers cannot be classified in terms of some fixed description of their actions. For example, a helper is not constantly acting in a prescriptive way. Sometimes helpers who work *predominantly* in a prescriptive way will find themselves being confronting or being informative. In many senses the skilled helper is one who is able to make effective use of the strategies of helping listed above in terms of the needs expressed and displayed by those who seek their help.

So helping is a dynamic process – it changes in response to events and circumstances. It is not a fixed body of skills. Whilst effective helping can be examined in terms of the skills a particular helper displays, mere possession of a body of knowledge and technical skills will not ensure that helping will take place. Effective helping and counselling are particular forms of human relationships which involve the helper in an active process of seeking to understand, respect and be genuine with the person they are seeking to help. As Carl Rogers, a leading American psychologist, has suggested, counselling and helping is not a professional activity, it is 'a way of being' with another person.

Strategies and tactics

Just as an effective helper seeks to bring appropriate strategies to bear upon the problems presented by the person in need, the effective helper is also able to use a variety of tactics when pursuing a particular strategy. A particular helping strategy is a collection of tactics which the helper can use to achieve a particular purpose. For example, the informative strategy can be pursued by a variety of tactics – giving verbal instructions, demonstrating to one person how another deals with a problem, or suggesting that a person reads a particular book or article. In contrast the confrontation strategy can be pursued by means of challenges, highlighting mismatches between verbal statements and the person's behaviour, or by providing direct feedback. Each of these individual ways of pursuing a given strategy is referred to as a tactic.

Helping individuals

So far the emphasis has been upon helping individuals. The various descriptions and definitions of helping imply that there are individuals who experience some difficulty or distress which leads them to seek support or information from another.

What assumptions can be made about the person in need? The first is that the person has volunteered to seek help: they are voluntary 'clients' of some helper. This is not always the case. For example, many patients in hospitals or pupils in school receive help as a requirement of their membership of the organization of which they are a part. Others receive help because a third party wants them to – for example, young children attending child guidance clinics are often involuntary 'clients' sent at the decision of their parents; sometimes, a relative is called in to give advice to an elderly person despite the fact that this elderly person has not sought and does not want the advice. Since the motivation of the person in need is crucial to the success of any helping enterprise the voluntary or involuntary nature of help-seeking is of considerable importance: a person sent to be helped is less likely to hold the helper in positive regard than the person who seeks to be helped.

There is a closely related type of help-seeking behaviour which helpers also need to be aware of. Sometimes people seek help so as to avoid making a decision or changing. For example, there are some couples who seek marriage guidance not so much because they want to change their relationship but because they want to avoid having to change their relationship: going to marriage guidance is a way of holding off a decision to get divorced. One young unemployed person sought the advice of professional careers guidance workers in seven different agencies so that he could show his parents he was doing something about being unemployed. In fact each piece of advice was ignored. This help-seeking behaviour was being used as a way of avoiding facing up to unemployment and its consequences.

So helpers need to examine the motives which people have for seeking their help. A failure to do this can lead helpers to undertake a great deal of work which is unlikely to lead to any positive outcome.

The helper also needs to know whether others are involved in the helping process. For example, say you are working to help a person who is experiencing sexual problems and they are also seeking the help of a doctor, a psychologist and a sex therapist. It might be the case that one of their problems is that they are receiving too much contradictory advice. The person may be using you to counteract the helping activities of another. There are clear boundaries between the roles of professional helpers and others who work as helping professionals. Some will refuse to work as a helper if the person in need is already seeking help from another helper. Others take a different view, and seek to co-operate with other helpers in a team approach to helping. The volunteer helper who works in a small organization may have a difficulty in identifying the precise role they can play in relation to other helpers. This is what makes the discussion of how people have come to be helped and what they expect to derive from the helping process important. It also makes it necessary for the helper to be explicit about the way in which they are going to work at the start of the helping process.

When the service being provided is an *information* service, then those seeking its help need to know that they cannot expect to obtain counselling or advocacy from that service. Such services, however, are generally well-equipped with the necessary information about how and where such services can be obtained. The helper has to know where an individual can be referred to if helping can best be provided by others. Helpers need to recognize their own limitations and the nature of the resources available in the community around them. This will ensure that:

- the person in need is provided with the help most appropriate to their needs
- the helper is protected from becoming involved with a helping process which is beyond their ability to cope
- there are good and frequent contacts between those involved in the helping process.

The process of referring a person in need from one helper to another must be undertaken with considerable care. All helping relationships are founded upon trust and mutual respect. A great many persons reveal to a helper information or feelings which they would not like to be revealed to someone else. The helper, in making a referral to another person, should do so with the consent and agreement of the person in need. They ought to brief the helper who is to work with the person as fully as possible but without disclosing information which that person has provided in confidence to the helper. Most of all, they need to motivate the person seeking help to actively want the referral to work – they should not feel that they are being dumped on or pushed over to someone else.

These comments about the task of helping an individual in need will be developed in other sections of this book. The point to note here is that they suggest that the helper has a significant role to play in determining the extent to which an attempt at helping is successful.

Helping in families and groups

Not all helping activity is concerned primarily with individuals. Some helpers work with families so as to change the way in which the family interacts. Such helping may be prompted by the needs of a particular family – for example, a girl who is anorexic or a boy who is bedwetting – but the helper's attention is upon the family as a unit rather than upon the individual who is displaying some 'symptom' of the family's problems. More details of this approach are given in the suggested readings at the end of the chapter. The intention here is to present ideas about helping which can be used in a variety of contexts, including family-focused helping.

Other helpers find themselves working with groups. For example, voluntary organizations run groups for those who wish to develop skills in assertiveness or wish to come to terms with bereavement; others run groups which are directed at mastering some social skill, such as problem-solving; yet others offer group courses on such diverse topics as 'managing stress', 'coming to terms with sexuality', 'growing up' or dealing with tranquillizers. Other helpers work for institutions – schools, colleges, Government training programmes – in which those in need are defined as organized groups. I am concerned with this form of helping, since in most cases the unit of concern which the helper has is the individual. In fact, a great many groups which offer helping resources in the community are concerned with individual needs; groups are organized because they are an economic and practical way of meeting the individual needs of a number of people simultaneously. Whilst there are some special skills for groupwork (examined more fully in Chapter 10), many of the skills and ideas to be described throughout this book are relevant to group based work aimed at helping individuals.

Helping and the community

The list of forms of helping did not describe *who* did these things, only what kinds of things were done in the name of helping. A great deal of helping activity takes place through organizations and professions which see themselves as concerned with communities rather than individuals. For example, neighbourhood law centres provide individuals with legal advice and support but they also assist in major community developments, such as co-ownership housing, the formation of charities, and advising on the legal aspects of social campaigns about such matters as pensions and child benefit. In this case, a neighbourhood law centre is helping individuals *and* a community.

To give another example, there are a number of co-operative development agencies funded by either Government or trades unions. A great deal of their time is spent helping groups of people develop a new co-operative or business. Such agencies also have an educational role and spend some of their time introducing people to the idea of co-operation for a variety of projects, not all of which are business-oriented. They can be said to be helping individuals through the promotion of particular co-operative projects and helping the community through the promotion of co-operation as a way of organizing activities that communities want.

Helping can thus be seen to be focused upon the individual (in the case of one-to-one helping or through groups), upon families, or upon the community. A voluntary organization, like Age Concern or the Samaritans, may find itself working at all three levels at different times. Helpers need to make conscious choices about these three kinds of work – individual, family or community – since different skills and attitudes are involved and the way in which the needs of a particular person are viewed will differ between them. Voluntary organizations which work at all three of these levels – as many do – need to identify consciously when helping an individual becomes a matter for helping a family or a focus for some community-based initiative. A lack of clarity about helping can lead the person in need to be used by the helper for purposes which they did not intend and subsequently feel manipulated into.

Helping is a process

The point made throughout this chapter in different ways is that there are a variety of helping forms and styles. I have provided some ways of thinking about them.

But helping is not something that can be easily fitted into one or other of the categories introduced here. On the contrary, helping is a complex, subtle and sometimes fraught process in which two or more people are genuinely in touch with each other and are seeking to effect some change. This change may be simple – from not having a clue where to find out about something to knowing about something – or it may be change that has dramatic implications for the way a person's life is led. But it is a change through a *process*. The remainder of this book is concerned with illuminating the processes of helping.

Suggested reading

Munro, E.A., Manthei, R.J. and Small, J.J. (1983) *Counselling – A Skills Approach*. New Zealand: Methuen.
An excellent introduction to counselling and helping skills. Full of practical advice and suggestions.
Nelson-Jones, R. (1983) *Practical Counselling Skills*. London: Holt, Rinehart and Winston.
An invaluable practical guide to counselling from a counselling psychology viewpoint. Includes a useful glossary and suggestions for practical activity.
Murgatroyd, S. and Woolfe, R. (1985) *Helping Families in Distress – An Introduction to Family Focussed Helping*. London: Harper and Row.
A thorough but not over-technical introduction to helping through the family. Illustrated throughout with case material and suggestions for practice.
Dryden, W. (ed.) (1984) *Individual Psychotherapy in Britain*. London: Harper and Row.
An excellent introductory text on psychotherapy and counselling. This book introduces different schools of counselling and therapy, each of which is described lucidly and succinctly and then illustrated with a case study. Includes some useful material on eclecticism.
Stewart, W. (1983) *Counselling for Nurses*. London: Lippincott.
An introductory text for health workers (especially nurses) aimed at showing the relevance of counselling and helping skills to work in medical settings.

Chapter 2

The Basic Features of
a Helping Relationship

Different skills are needed for the different kinds of helping outlined in the previous chapter. These will be examined throughout the book. Before looking at some of these skills it is necessary for you to understand and explore some of the basic features of a helping relationship which can make all the difference between success and failure.

Carl Rogers – a leading figure in counselling – has suggested that helpers need to communicate three basic qualities if a helping relationship is to be successful: *empathy, warmth,* and *genuineness.* He suggests that the helper's ability to communicate these qualities would be sufficient to determine whether or not a helping relationship would have a positive outcome. Let me now examine each of these conditions in turn.

Empathy

One dictionary defines empathy as 'the power or state of imagining oneself to be another person and so of sharing his ideas and feelings' (Longman's Dictionary). But Rogers provides a more accurate definition. Empathy, according to Carl Rogers, is the ability to experience another person's world as if it were one's own without ever losing that 'as if' quality.

It is important to understand that empathy is not the same as sympathy – they are quite different. Sympathy involves offering another person support and emotional comfort because they are in some distress or pain; empathy involves entering the private world of another person so as to understand that world, irrespective of whether sympathy is offered or not. It is also important to recognize that the nature of empathy is different from the nature of *role.* What is involved in understanding another person's role as, say, a patient in pain, a woman experiencing divorce, a child going into care, or a husband recently bereaved is an understanding of the *general* condition of being in that role. Empathy involves the helper being sensitive, moment to moment, to the changing experience of the *particular* person one is seeking to help. Empathy is particular, not general; it is about understanding and sharing, not judging and supporting. Empathy requires you to enter the world of another person 'as if' it were your own so that you can better understand what it is like to be that person in need of your help.

None of this is easy. Indeed, it is very difficult to achieve a state of total empathy with another person, especially if time is short and you are trying to listen and attend to them in the midst of others. But it is important to constantly aim at the goal of achieving accurate empathy. A failure to communicate empathy will lead the person in need to think of you as not understanding or not recognizing what he or she is going through, or not caring.

The idea that empathy is a condition or frame of mind to aim at has some practical implications for helping. First it implies that you should check out what the person in need is saying to you so that you can check your understanding of what is being said and show that you recognize its meaning for the person. This is known as *reflection of content*. Here are three examples:

Leon: I don't know how to make a good impression on people ...
Helper: You say you don't make a good impression on people. Who specifically do you fail to make a good impression on?
Leon: I don't know, I mean whenever I try to get help or try to make friends, I don't know, I just seem to fail to make a good impression on people, period.
Helper: You say that you fail to get help from people or to make friends because you fail to make a good impression on them ... you say this seems always to be the case?
Leon: Well, I don't know, it seems to me that I don't even make a good impression on my mother ...

In this example the helper reflects back to Leon the meaning of what he has said using the words Leon himself used.

Sally: I get really angry when I think of just what is happening here. Do you realize that I have been passed up for promotion and then I have been asked to take additional duties without extra pay!

Well, I tell you, I am not going to stand for it ... I am not going to be pushed around like a rotten egg in a salad.

Helper: You feel pushed around because you feel used, is that how you feel – angry, pushed around and used?

In this example the helper summarizes the content through a question which is intended to show both that he had been listening and that he wanted to check out his understanding before proceeding.

Mike: I am in a lot of pain about Jackie leaving. Sometimes it's physical – I feel sick and I feel exhausted and I get headaches. Most times it's pain right down in my guts somewhere. I mean real pain. It's like when my mother died – I just felt helpless and lost and broken ...

Helper: Just as you felt when you lost your mother, Jackie's leaving you has left you helpless and in pain.

Mike: Yeah, real pain ... *(starts to cry)* I don't know if I can cope with all this pain again ... I nearly died myself when mother died and now Jackie's gone and I just feel washed-up, like a fish on dry land gasping for air. I don't know if I can cope ...

Helper: The loss of these two women seems to mean the same thing for you, Mike – pain and a feeling that you're not going to cope.

Mike: Yeah, yeah that's right ...

In this last example the helper seeks to communicate his understanding through the immediate reflection back of the principal content.

A second practical implication of the attempt to achieve and communicate empathy concerns *reflection of feelings*. When reflecting content the aim is to check that the message the person is offering is accurately understood. But in the reflection of feeling the aim is to check that the underlying and often *implicit* emotions that *accompany* the expression of content are also understood. Now this is much more difficult. There are literally thousands of adjectives and phrases available to describe feelings like 'anxious' (for example, tense, nervous, panic-stricken, stressed, worried, deeply concerned, frightened) or 'depressed' (for example, sad, blue, unhappy, feeling low). Each of these adjectives or phrases carries slightly different meanings, the nuance of which might just be crucial to the person you are helping. Just as you should aim to accurately reflect content, you should also aim to accurately communicate your understanding of the emotions which accompany such content. Here are three examples:

Helper: You say you are concerned about what you will feel like after the operation to remove your breast.

Mary: Yes, I mean all sorts of complications could set in, but ... well, will I look ugly, you know to my husband, you know, er, ... will he still want me ... Will it affect me in any way other than physically ... you know, you hear so much about hysterectomy affecting women – they get depressed and anxious ... will this, this operating do the same ...

Helper: I hear you say 'Will I be the same emotionally and sexually after the operation ...'

Mary: Well, yes that's it ... what the hell's it going to do to me?

Helper: I also hear a lot of anxiety in your voice ...

Notice in this example that the medical social worker who is acting as the helper uses both the content of what Mary says and the way in which Mary says the words as a basis for her reaction. Often the tone of voice, the way the person fidgets or looks can reveal as much as (and sometimes more than) the words that are used. This is also the case in the next example:

June: I don't know how to say this, but I'm scared of my husband ... I just don't know if I can cope with him any more. Don't get me wrong, he's not hit me or anything ... I just think he might. The other day, for instance, he was upset that his tea wasn't ready when he came in ... he never said how are you or anything ... (I had been to the doctor's and I hadn't been well ...), he was just angry ... really angry.

Helper: You feel threatened, anxious and a little puzzled ... you also sound and look as if you are not quite sure about the kind of person you married.

June: You've got it!

In this final example, which is a little longer than the previous two, the helper deliberately focuses upon what the person in need leaves vague:

Sam: I will not be able to do the exam tomorrow, I, I just don't feel that, well, I am ready ...

Helper: You say that you do not *feel* ready for tomorrow's exam ... what do you feel like right now?

Sam: Well, I am angry with myself that I'm going to have to quit this exam and, well ... I guess I'm anxious...

Helper: You guess that you are anxious ...

Sam: Well, I am anxious... very anxious ...

Helper: You don't guess that you are anxious you know that you feel very anxious. When you think about this anxiety, what image do you have of yourself?

Sam: Well, (*looks sheepish and unhappy*) I see myself trying to explain to my Dad why I didn't make the grade on this course ... and I see him getting angry ... and, well, I start to feel like I have let him down again.

Helper: You don't feel ready for your exam, you feel anxious and you don't want to let your Dad down *again.* Tell me about the last time you let your Dad down.

Sam: Oh, well, it was a year ago ... He'd entered me for a chess competition and I got knocked out in the first match ... he was angry because he'd told all his friends just how good I was ...

Helper: What did you tell him ... as an explanation when you lost the chess game?

Sam: I told him (*looks as if he makes a connection at the level of his feelings*) that I wasn't ready to play in the league.

Helper: And now you are preparing to tell him that you are not ready to sit this examination.

(*45 seconds of silence*)

Sam: Yes, I suppose I am.

Helper: How would you know if you were ready? What would you feel like, what would you be saying to yourself?

Sam: (*looks surprised at the question*) Well, I guess I wouldn't be worried ... I'd feel confident that I could answer any question asked of me ... and I'd feel sure that I could get a really good grade.

Helper: Sam, how many other students do you know who *are* going to sit the exam tomorrow and feel the way you have just described?

Sam: None, actually.

Helper: So, Sam, none of the students you know who are actually going to sit the exam tomorrow are feeling ready for it. Despite this, they are going to sit the exam. Why are you so different, Sam?

Sam: (*tearful*) Well ... I guess they don't have my father to contend with.

Helper: OK, Sam, let's recognize that you are saying to me that you feel reluctant to take the exam tomorrow because you do not like the thought of having to explain away a poor grade or a failure to your father if this is how it turns out, is that right Sam?

Sam: Shit. That's it in a nutshell.

ample, the helper managed to use what Sam implied as a
a more accurate statement of the problem. This new state-
gives both Sam and his helper something concrete to work on
connects the concern Sam is now expressing with his past and
his future.

Developing empathy skills

There are some practical steps a helper can take to develop skills in
empathy. These include:

- Practise reflecting content with other people – friends at work and
  at home, relatives, family. Try to reflect back what they have said
  (paraphrase) and check your understanding.
- Try to imagine someone you are helping in the various situations
  which they describe to you as if you were making a documentary
  video. Try to create as accurate a picture as you can on this screen
  of the experiences they describe.
- If you do not think visually, imagine the person as the key character in a novel you are reading or writing – think of all the phrases
  to describe this person and the situations they outline to you. I
  find it particularly helpful to think of myself writing their
  biography.
- Work on increasing your vocabulary of emotions – use diction-
  aries, a thesaurus, novels and films and any other materials you
  can to enrich the way you can describe what a feeling is like.

By undertaking these tasks (and others you might devise yourself)
you will find yourself gradually able to increase the extent to which
you can communicate your empathy accurately with others.

Warmth

The second feature of helping which Carl Rogers regarded as essential was something called 'unconditional positive regard'. Other
words for this feature are *acceptance* or *warmth*.

In coining the term 'unconditional positive regard' Carl Rogers
wished helpers and counsellors to *'prize the person'* – to respect
people for what they are, for their uniqueness and for their individu-
ality. He wished helpers to begin their relationship with a person by
directly communicating that you accept them, no matter how they
might speak or what they might have done. Another way of thinking
about this condition is to regard it as requiring helpers to create a climate within which the person in need can feel safe.

Why did Carl Rogers attach such importance to this condition for change and effective helping? His argument goes something like this:

- a person in need has come to you for help
- in order to be helped they need to know that you understand how they think and feel
- they also need to know that, whatever your own feelings about who or what they are or about what they have or have not done, you accept them as they are – you accept their right to decide their own lives for themselves
- in the light of this knowledge about your acceptance and understanding of them they will begin to open themselves to the possibility of change and development
- but if they feel that their association with you is conditional upon them changing, they may then feel pressured and reject your help.

To illustrate the idea of warmth, here is a transcript of the first few minutes of an interview between Mary and a school counsellor – Mary is 17.

Mary: So, here I am then, great, fuck!

Helper: Here you are, Mary.

Mary: Have you any idea what's been happening to me, eh? Any idea at all?

Helper: Mary, all I know is that you have asked to see me and that you seem anxious.

Mary: Anxious, fuck me, I'm anxious. Shit, I'm anxious. Look, I am so anxious I feel that I could scream my head off. Christ! I mean Christ!

Helper: Tell me about what's happening to you, Mary. I'd like to know.

Mary: (stands up and paces the room, looks anxious) Look, everything I say here, right, I mean it's just between you and me, right. I mean no other bugger is going to know, right?

Helper: I'll stop you from getting to a point where I might have to tell others, so yes.

Mary: Well, I mean this is serious – I mean fucking serious.

Helper: I see and hear how serious it is for you, Mary.

Mary: OK, now this is it – I don't want no lectures or sermons, right, but I've got venereal disease. Don't ask me who, don't ask me when, but I've got it ... and I tell you, it's enough to send a woman gay!

Helper: You have a venereal disease and you feel upset and vulnerable. I can see that and hear that. Tell me, Mary, so far who else have you told?

Mary: No one. I don't want no one else to know either. I came to you because I just had to tell someone. You probably think I'm a slut or just a piece of ass willing to put-out for anyone, I'm not like that, honest, but I've got landed with the pox and everyone will treat me like a whore, I know, I just know ...

Helper: Am I treating you like a whore right now, Mary?

Mary: Well, no, no you're not.

Mary is clearly already upset and feeling vulnerable. The helper does not interrupt her or caution her about her use of language or pass a moral judgement on her behaviour. The helper seeks to understand and to communicate care, concern and warmth to Mary. An attempt to stop her 'bad' language might have meant that Mary had no one with whom she could share her feelings. The helper here shows a great deal of acceptance.

Notice that the helper in this example did not behave like Mary in order to gain acceptance. Nor was the helper pretending to accept Mary when in fact she did not. Acceptance is about communicating the warmth you actually feel for a person in need. There is no suggestion here that, in order to achieve warmth, you need to be passive or bland, or aggressively intimate with the person in need; rather, there is a need to respect them directly through active listening, the communication of empathy, sharing insights and observations and valuing their opinions, thoughts, feelings and observations.

A final word here. Warmth is a frame of mind, not a practical skill. There are no easy clues as to how to develop this frame of mind – no practical exercises or skill tests one can complete. Showing warmth to others comes from developing relationships with others in which both you and they feel that you are there to learn from each other – you are seeking their respect and acceptance and exercise the 'power' of being a helper consciously, having careful regard for its impact on others. The importance of warmth is that it creates a climate within which change can take place.

Genuineness

The third condition outlined by Carl Rogers as necessary for effective helping and counselling is genuineness, though some writers prefer the term *authenticity*. Like warmth, this is a difficult construct to define and explain.

The simplest way of thinking about genuineness is to regard it as open communication. Instead of the person in need trying to guess at what you really mean, or trying to decode the differences between what you say and the image your body communication provides them with, there is a directness and openness about the way you communicate. You are not presenting an image of a 'super-helper', you are yourself as you genuinely feel at that time. What is more, you are encouraging the person in need to communicate this way too. You encourage them to stop pretending, denying, hiding, concealing their thoughts and feelings – you encourage direct and open communication. To do this you provide them with an example – your own open communication.

An interesting point arises from this way of thinking about genuineness: the behaviour of a helper when working with someone in need is no different from the way they behave when they are working with a colleague on some joint project, or working with a member of their family on some issue of concern to them both. Helping is a way of being, not simply a role that is performed between (say) 9 am and 5 pm. Though a helper will work at different levels of intensity at different times, genuineness will need to be present if effective helping is to take place.

Thinking of genuineness as a statement of open communication suggests another link with warmth. A common difficulty in thinking about warmth is the feeling that it inevitably involves the suppression of the thoughts and feelings of the helper. However, when all three conditions are taken together – empathy, warmth *and* genuineness – it is clear that the helper is in a position to share thoughts and feelings with the person in need, providing that they are aiming to understand what the inner world of that person is like, and that their comments and reactions to them as a person are founded upon their acceptance of and warmth towards that person. Rather than just being a careful listener, passively accepting the world of the person in need, the addition of this condition of genuineness opens out the helping process to being one in which the helper can share and openly express themselves just as much as the person in need. Indeed, the helper is here recognized as a person with their own needs when engaged in helping others.

Let me illustrate the way in which genuineness can be experienced in a helping relationship through two examples. The first is a transcript of a part of my own work with a chronically depressed person:

Chris: I just can't see a way forward, Steve ... everything I think of is full of problems.

Helper: Chris, I have sat here for six weeks now working with you. I have the feeling that if I just asked you to sit in another chair in this room you'd find about 17 reasons why this would be difficult for you.

Chris: Are you angry with me?

Helper: Not so much angry, Chris, as frustrated.

Chris: Oh dear, now I am making you unhappy ...

Helper: Stop, Chris. Just listen to what you have just said. You are concerned that you are making me unhappy. I am not unhappy. I am frustrated. I am not frustrated just with you hanging on to your depression – I am also frustrated with me being unable to shift you right now. Let's try something. I want you to imagine how I feel right now, Chris ... what do you think is passing through my mind.

Chris: I think you think I am useless and helpless and that I will always be like this ...

Helper: Chris, I don't think that. I think that you are very able to do many of the things you want to do, but I think you stop yourself by assuming that you will fail.

Chris: Yes, that's how I think.

Helper: Right, I feel as if I have made some progress for me ... I have let something out about the way I feel about you. Chris, how do you feel about you?

Chris: Oh, alright most of the time.

Helper: You mean, you feel alright about being depressed most of the time?

Chris: (smiling) Oh, you get used to it ...

This illustration of the helper offering a genuine reflection to the person he is helping was productive in this session – Chris disclosed that the depression was something he found comfortable. Later, this was to be used as a basis for some drama work with Chris. The point to note is that the helper did not shrink from disclosing his own frustration and made sure that the person he was helping was clear in his understanding of the nature of this frustration. Being genuine in this way means that the helper can be open rather than closed in communications; they can be spontaneous with a person rather than pre-programmed or rehearsed; they can express their own thoughts and feelings rather than hide them.

The second example comes from the work of a nurse-counsellor working with a cancer patient in a hospice.

Sally: Nurse, will I be able to see a specialist tomorrow, there's something important I need to ask him.

Helper: I think that can be arranged, Sally. Meantime, can I help?

Sally: Well, well ... I know I am dying and that there's no real hope. I know it will take between a month and a year to happen, and I just don't want to sit here waiting to die. I want him to give me something, you know, so that I'll go to sleep and not wake up ... I hear some of these doctors will do that.

Helper: I don't think you'll find Mr Higshaw like that and you should think of others, too.

Sally: Like who? I haven't got any relatives. No sons or daughters to weep over me. I might just as well be dead.

Helper: Oh really! And what about me and Nurse Fitzgibbon? Don't we count as people who will weep when you do die?

Sally: Oh you, it's just a job to you, isn't it, just a job?

Helper: This is my job, Sally. But it isn't just a job. I work here because I want to. I want to be a part of someone's life, especially those like yourself who have no one else to care and worry with them. I want to ensure that everyone in this place knows that someone will give their time and their heart to them. And I will cry when you go, Sally, just like I cried when Maud died yesterday. I am not your daughter, Sally, I know that, but I do care. Don't just dismiss that as being my job.

Sally: Oh don't get all sentimental – why should you care about some old fuddy duddy who'll be gone in a few weeks?

Helper: There are lots of reasons, Sally. But I'll give you two. One is that I could just as easily be lying where you are – cancer affects a large number of people and it could be me. The other reason, Sally, is that I have been through times when I felt despair and wanted to die and end it all – and someone held my hand at the right time.

Sally: (after a pause) Do you really care about me, I mean, it's not just a job?

Helper: (holding Sally's hand) Yes, Sally, I do ... this is not just a job. I will cry for you.

Self-disclosure, as used here, can show that the helper is in tune both with their own thoughts and feelings and those of the person in need. Genuineness can also be regarded as a way of expressing authentic feelings for a person.

Like warmth, genuineness is not a skill that can be acquired through training or avid reading – it is a feature of the way a helper is and can be with others. It is not a statement about something a helper chooses to *do*, rather it is a statement of how they choose to *be* in their relationships with others.

Having made this observation, there are ways in which you can improve the extent to which you can communicate your genuineness to others. Four suggestions are made here:

- develop the ability to describe yourself to yourself – pay particular attention to changes in your mood, your relationships with others, and your strengths and weaknesses
- develop your ability to describe yourself to others – practise self-disclosure
- read books about personal psychology and read about self-concept and personality and examine your own thinking, feelings and behaviours in the light of this reading
- try to predict your own behaviour – see just how good a judge of your own character and reactions you are and examine why it is that you sometimes react in ways which you did not intend.

The aim of these activities is to encourage you to act in ways that facilitate self-disclosure, encourage honesty and improve self-understanding. It is important that these features of yourself are examined, since much of the helping process involves asking those in need to perform exactly these tasks.

Other basic features of helping

When Carl Rogers suggested that empathy, warmth and genuineness were *necessary* conditions for effective helping and counselling, he also suggested that these 'core conditions' (as they are now known) were *sufficient* to secure significant changes for a person. A great deal of research supports his proposition that these conditions are necessary, but few now support his contention that they are sufficient. Indeed, many researchers have been able to identify a number of other features which appear necessary for effective helping. One particular researcher, Robert Carkhuff, has identified three other commonly observed features of helping and has suggested that these features – *concreteness*, *immediacy*, and *confrontation* – need also to be regarded as necessary and basic conditions for helping.

Concreteness

The image the term 'concreteness' creates in many people's minds of a man or woman stuck in drying concrete is not the image Cark-huff intended to convey when he first used this term. It implies *specificity* – the helper seeks to ensure that the person in need is being specific about the meaning they attach to the terms he or she uses to express ideas, images, thoughts or feelings and that their description of events is accurate. Here is an example of a helper trying to get Barry to be concrete.

Barry: When I'm asked to do this (*work at studying for his examinations*) I just get bored.

Helper: Bored. When you feel bored, just how do you feel and what do you do?

Barry: Well, I sit around and just sort of do nothing.

Helper: When you sit around and do nothing, are you saying anything to yourself ... are you using any kind of self-conversation?

Barry: Yeah, I'm kind of saying, er, like I've done this before and I don't think I like having to do it again.

Helper: Can you express this thought as if it were happening now?

Barry:...er ... God I'm bored ... I've looked at all this stuff before and I didn't like it then...and here I am again...there must be better things to do with my time than this ... God, I'm bored.

Helper: What would happen if you were to say to yourself ... 'I can do better things with my time once I have finished this work'...?

Barry: I think I'd get frustrated.

Helper: Is being frustrated different from being bored for you?

Barry: Well, I don't know ...

Helper: Think about it, Barry ... are you saying that you get frustrated about having to work because it prevents you from doing something you really want to do, or are you saying that you are just bored?

Barry: I think that I'm really saying that all this work is frustrating.

Helper: OK, Barry. Now how else is not completing this work going to be frustrating to you?

Barry: What do you mean?

Helper: If you don't complete this work what else will you be denying yourself?

Barry: Ah ... I see ... well, I guess I'll be denying myself some of my summer and a lot of my evenings if I fail the exam that's coming up in two weeks ... I'll also be denying myself peace and quiet at home ... there'll be a lot of aggro.

Helper: OK, so you feel frustrated right now but can see how much

more you will be frustrated in the future if you don't work right now.
Barry: Yeah, awesome, eh?

Being concrete requires the helper to ensure that the person in need is conveying the exact meaning of the situation which they are experiencing and their reactions to it. It involves the helper asking questions such as:

'... what do you mean by ...?'
'... when you say you feel ... can you be more specific about this feeling ...?'
'... how do others react to you when you say you are feeling this way?'

A failure to engage the person in need in this concrete way implies that the helper is willing to guess that the terms used by that person mean the same to both of them. Yet experience suggests that this is rarely the case. For example, the simple question 'Are you in pain?' means different things to different people – largely because individuals have different pain thresholds. The statement 'I am in love' has a great many different meanings. Helpers need to be concerned to understand the exact meaning of key terms and ideas as expressed by the person in need.

For many kinds of helpers – most especially those concerned with advice giving and the offering of support – the quality of concreteness is critical in determining the success of a helping relationship. Advice givers need to check that their understanding of the question asked of them matches that of the person they are advising; those seeking to facilitate some emotional release need to understand accurately the meanings of the emotional words used by the person; support givers need to understand in a definite sense how that person has come to see them as a source of support. So being concrete and specific is essential to the task of helping.

Immediacy

Those in need spend a great deal of time describing to the helper some feature of their past or imagined future. For example, a couple seeking marriage guidance will typically talk at length about their behaviour towards each other in the past and the consequences of changing (or not changing) their behaviours for the future. One task the helper has is to encourage them to focus upon the immediate relationship – the 'here and now'. This is a central feature of a great many helping situations.

When a person in need is preoccupied with the past and the future, it is difficult for them to examine how they think and feel *right now*. All current behaviour becomes measured in terms of past and future. Descriptions of actual events become locked into past events and future hopes. The result is a lack of honesty about self and poor levels of self-disclosure; this is often accompanied by poor interpersonal skills and a lack of social awareness. The helper who seeks to affect these features of the person in need will need to encourage them to talk about their thoughts and feelings *as they happen* and discourage them from thinking of past and future all the time. Here is an example from my work with an anxious woman.

Sharon: I never used to be like this – you know, worried all the time about what others might think or about, well, everything really ...
Helper: Are you worried right now, Sharon?
Sharon: You mean about what we talked about – about moving house and changing my job, oh yes, I can see all sorts of problems on the horizon, I mean ...
Helper: (interrupting) No, Sharon, I don't mean about moving and changing jobs, I mean right here and now in this room as you talk to me – are you anxious *now*?
Sharon: I wasn't until you asked me to think about it ...
Helper: Describe how you feel right now ...
Sharon: I don't know really.
Helper: Sharon, I am not asking you to be right, I am asking you just to describe how you feel right now in as much detail as possible. Do it, Sharon, I know you can do it.
Sharon: Well (coughs) I feel sweaty and nervous and, well, like teetering on the edge of something, like I was going to fall or something.
Helper: You feel you are going to fall, concentrate on that feeling, Sharon, and tell me what image you have of yourself right now.
Sharon: I see myself hung on a wire and the wire is twisted and broken – I am holding on by a thread. I am frightened that you will cut me off and I will fall.

Immediacy is achieved here by requiring the person in need to share their experiences of being in the helping relationship as it is happening. The quality of this work, when it works well, is well worth the effort it involves.

Another way of describing immediacy is to say that it is a term used to describe spontaneous self-disclosure. The helper is seeking to encourage the person to be honest with themselves, to reflect upon their thoughts and feelings as they occur and to see the present (the 'here and now') as a meaningful focus for their thoughts and feelings. Here is an extract from a later meeting I had with Sharon – about eight months after the first extract:

Sharon: Sometimes I feel angry with you, Steve.

Helper: Tell me about the things that make you angry, Sharon.

Sharon: No, I don't want to tell you about the things that make me angry, I want to tell you about what it feels like to be angry.

Helper: Hm, hm.

Sharon: When I feel angry with you I have two feelings – I've only recently noticed the second one. The first feeling is of frustration. I feel frustrated that I am still having to come to see you, though I recognize that I am considerably less anxious than I have ever been before in my life. But I am angry that you can't work quicker. The other feeling is that I am glad that I can get angry with you – it means I feel more real as a person than I did before.

Helper: In what way do you feel more 'real' right now?

Sharon: I think I feel more real just because I am experiencing a greater range of feelings than I did before ... I guess I am also sharing them more, which I find not threatening now, but liberating ...

Notice that there is a significant change in both what Sharon is now saying and how she is saying it – I hope that the extract conveys her increased self-confidence and assurance.

Apart from encouraging spontaneous self-disclosure and enabling the person to improve social relationships, immediacy encourages the person and the helper to engage in open communication. For if the person in need is being asked to be genuine, to share thoughts and feelings as they occur, and to explore openly and honestly with the helper the meaning that they give to the helping relationship, then a basis for open communication is being established. The helper needs to reciprocate on equal terms, thus increasing the depth and intensity of the helping process. Immediacy is thus aided by the helper behaving in the same way that they ask the person in need to behave.

Immediacy is important to all forms of helping. The advice-giver needs to check that the person has understood the advice given and to monitor their reactions as the advice is being given so that further advice needs might be identified. The helper offering direction (for example, a nurse helping a patient cope with post-operative pain) needs to have a clear understanding of how that person is thinking and feeling right now. In the facilitative forms of helping, immediacy is the central feature of the relationship between the helper and the helped – in some of these forms it is the central feature of helping, as will be seen.

Confrontation

'Confrontation' does not imply any aggressiveness on the part of the helper. It refers to the helper's task of pointing out discrepancies between the helper's view of the person in need and their own. Confrontation usually involves one or more of three types of discrepancy:

- differences between the real and the ideal self of the person in need
- differences between what the person thinks and feels and what the person actually does
- differences between the real world as seen by the helper and the fantasy world as seen by the person in need.

The first discrepancy is the difference between that which a person *wishes* to become (the ideal self) and that which they *already* appear to be (the real self). Here are three examples:

> Miranda is 17 and doing averagely well at school. Despite average grades, Miranda sees herself to be exceptional and gifted. She has applied for a scholarship, even though she does not qualify by the rules for entry.
>
> Harry is 50 and has been retired through ill health from his work as a carpenter. Despite medical advice to the contrary and the evidence of his own body, Harry still thinks of himself as active and capable of performing the work he has always done.
>
> Arnold is 22 and a recent graduate in psychology from a British university. Though he graduated with a below-average degree, he has established himself as a consulting psychologist and is seeking now to attract large contracts for consultancy work from international companies. He boasts to his friends about his successful start in the world of commerce, despite the fact that after six months he has not secured a single day's consultancy work.

In these examples, the purpose of a confrontation by a helper would be to illuminate the extent and nature of the discrepancy in a way that can lead to change.

What is a discrepancy of thinking and feeling on the one hand and behaviour on the other? Here are three examples:

Muriel says that she is a confident and assertive person, yet each time she is challenged in any way she becomes quiet and upset. She is not as confident as she says she is.

Arthur claims that he never gets stressed by examinations, despite the fact that he has lost weight and has taken to smoking 20 cigarettes a day. His behaviour shows that he is anxious, despite his brave words.

Tricia says that she cannot stand her husband Brian any more and that she finds him despicable – yet she still makes love to him and boasts of her marriage to her neighbours and friends.

In these kinds of circumstances the helper needs to take full account of the likely impact of their intervention upon the thoughts, feelings and behaviours of the person in need. Such interventions need to be firmly rooted in empathy and warmth, since their impact is usually considerable.

The final discrepancy is between the *real* and *fantasy* world of the person in need. For example, adult education counsellors sometimes find themselves presented with a person who wishes to become a doctor at the age of 40, despite the fact that he or she has no experience of medicine and a poor academic record. So convinced are they by their own ability that they have already bought the textbooks and equipment a medical student might need! In such cases, the image the person has of themselves has taken over from the reality of their situation. In another example, marriage guidance counsellors sometimes find themselves discussing a marriage with one partner who is overly optimistic about the future, in spite of clear signs from the other partner that the marriage has ended and the real task is now one of conciliation rather than reconciliation. The unreality or fantasy view of self held by the person in need in these circumstances is often self-damaging in some way. Consider the girl who weighed eight and a half stones who felt very much over-weight and who, despite being under-weight for her height, was not eating and was taking laxatives in large quantities so as to reduce her weight. She was doing considerable damage to her stomach as well as creating increasingly tense interpersonal relationships at home.

Confrontation is a powerful feature of genuine helping relationships. It has to arise out of the development of an empathic and warm relationship in which the genuineness of the helper has been clearly and effectively established. Effective confrontation can accelerate the process of helping and counselling; conversely, an ineffective and inappropriate confrontation can considerably impair or lead to a premature ending of a helping relationship.

Here is an example of a confrontation. Suzy is a 23-year-old who is having difficulty making relationships with men:

Suzy: ... they're only after one thing.

Helper: ... what is it that they are all after?

Suzy: They all want sex with me. I could have lots of friends if I took my clothes off and let them at it.

Helper: Who specifically could you have as a friend if you agreed to have sex?

Suzy: Anyone, I could have men all the time.

Helper: Who specifically has told you or made clear to you that he would be your friend if you had sex with him?

Suzy: Well, no one's said look if you let me have sex with you then I'll be your friend, come on! But I know that this is what they think.

Helper: How do you know?

Suzy: I just do, everyone knows.

Helper: I am a man, Suzy, do you think that I am like all the men you are talking about?

Suzy: No, no of course not ... you are different.

Helper: How do you know, Suzy?

Suzy: Well, I don't know just how, I only know that you're different.

Helper: OK, Suzy – who else do you know that's different?

Suzy: Well (*thinks carefully*), Frank's different. Yeah, Frank.

Helper: Frank is a man at work, eh?

Suzy: Yeah ... he works in our office.

Helper: Why is Frank different?

Suzy: Well, he's older.

Helper: So older men don't want to offer friendship to you in return for sex?

Suzy: (*hesitantly*) ... well ...

Helper: You don't seem too sure about any of this, Suzy. It seems to me like you have no real evidence that your friendship with other people is conditional on you having sex with them. It seems to me to be clear that you have started to believe something that either you fear or you wish to be true. I don't think you make relationships with men because you are afraid that it will lead to you having sex with them.

Suzy: (cries) Oh, God. I just want to have friends and all I do is attract the guys who want to screw.

Helper: ... and you don't?

Suzy: Well, sometimes ... but I don't want to have to screw just so I can have friends.

Helper: I think it's only you that tells yourself that you have to screw so as to have friends.

This extract shows that the confrontation is based upon an assessment of the way the person is thinking. What it does not convey, though it is clear on the audio-tape from which this is transcribed, is that the confrontation is gentle and not coercive – the tone of voice and manner of the helper were supportive and not combative.

The helping relationship

Six basic features of a helping relationship – empathy, warmth, genuineness, concreteness, immediacy and confrontation – have now been described. These six elements are present in all helping relationships to some degree. They are necessary or basic features of helping. They are not so much descriptions of helping skills, but statements of the way in which one person (the helper) seeks to be when engaged in the task of helping a person in need.

But how does the person in need view the helping relationship? What do we know about the way in which those who seek help view the helping process?

Barbara Berzon listed eight features of helping which reflect the characteristics of helping most valued by those who have been helped:

- *Increased awareness* – being encouraged to increase self-understanding and to learn more about the ways others see them.
- *Recognition of similarity* – being shown how similar they were in many respects to others, something especially important to those who seek help precisely because they feel out of touch with others.
- *Core conditions* – the extent to which the person feels that they are understood, accepted and reacted to genuinely by their helper.
- *Self–other perception* – being made aware how others see them.
- *Expressiveness* – being encouraged to self-disclose, to be assertive and to be immediate in their reactions.
- *Open communication* – those being helped appreciated the open-

ness and warmth of helper communication, even when the helper was confrontative.

● *Warmth* – those helpers who are themselves and do not play the role of helper are most respected by those with whom they work.

● *Ventilation* – help seekers appreciate the opportunity to share and divulge inner thoughts and feelings in a safe and neutral atmosphere.

These eight points express succinctly much of what has gone before in this chapter from the point of view of the person being helped. Helpers have to be themselves and engage in the helping process with a high level of energy and commitment. By engaging in the helping process in this way, the helper acts as a model for the person in need to follow. Finally, the helper's prime function is to encourage the person in need to self-disclose, discover options and engage in interaction honestly with other people. This listing of Burzon's findings summarizes the basic features of effective helping relationships.

Suggested reading

Rogers, C.R. (1961) *On Becoming a Person.* Boston: Houghton-Mifflin.
A major text by Carl Rogers. Though it is a long book – 420 pages – it is broken down into manageable doses which are easy to read. It is not over-technical. Essential reading for those who see themselves as counsellors.

Tough, A. (1982) *Intentional Changes – A Fresh Approach to Helping People Change.* Chicago: Follett Publishing.
An easy to read and imaginative account of change conditions by one of Canada's leading adult educators. An invaluable source of materials and ideas for all engaged in helping activity, especially within educational settings.

Chapter 3

Being Helped

We have now explored different forms and strategies for helping and the basic conditions for helping which contribute to the quality of helping and counselling relationships. I now examine the expectations of the person in need, together with the idea that certain forms of helping are more effective for some than for others. The issues discussed in the two previous chapters are looked at from a different viewpoint: that of the 'customer' or 'client', as the person in need is often called.

Counsellor and client matching

The way in which a person in need approaches a helper depends critically upon the nature of their needs. For example, a woman with an acute vaginal problem who suspects that she has a venereal disease will approach a doctor of either sex but is reluctant to approach a male counsellor. Similarly, men who seek marriage counselling favour male counsellors, especially if the marital problem they are seeking to resolve involves sexual difficulties. These examples suggest that the sex of the person in need sometimes needs to be matched to the sex of the helper.

This is referred to as 'gender matching' by psychologists, and applies more strongly in some cultures than others. For example, in cultures which are patriarchal – such as many Middle Eastern cultures – a man rarely discusses his personal difficulties with a woman. In addition, gender matching is more important for some kinds of needs. Sexual difficulties have been mentioned as one example of need where gender matching is desirable; another area is the development of assertiveness, where women show a clear preference for assertiveness training to be undertaken by women rather than men (see Chapter 5).

Just as the need to match the helper's gender with that of the person in need is sometimes important, so too is the need for the helper to be identified with the prevailing culture of that person. A personal illustration may make this point clearly. During my training as a crisis counsellor I spent time working in a crisis centre in a black district of New York. I was the only white person on the staff team and, as if this was not enough of a difference, I was British and not American and spoke with a different accent from my clients. I was also relatively young (a little over 30) and they were all older than I was. These differences did not prevent me working in this culture. But they made the work more difficult for both those in need and myself since the use of colloquial expressions, local idioms, shared knowledge and a common basis of local history was difficult and often impossible. When doctors talk to their patients as if they (the patients) had received the same medical education the same problem arises – symptoms and treatments are described in technical terms and the patient is left feeling most unsure as to the precise nature of their illness and the course of treatment they are expected to follow. Thus the culture matching of the person in need and their helper is desirable for maximum effectiveness – the term 'culture' being used to refer to social background.

Gender and culture matching between the helper and the person in need are desirable because the person in need seeks to relate at as many levels as possible to the person who is helping them. They wish to feel understood not simply because they have described their need to the helper but because they feel that their need could have arisen in the life of the helper. Notice the use of the word 'could' here: the person in need often wishes to imagine their helper in their situation. This is made more difficult if the differences between the helper and the person in need are considerable.

Competence

Next in the list of qualities of helpers which those in need look for is confidence in their helper's competence. Counsellors and helpers are expected by their clients to know what it is they are doing; to feel confident about their ability to work with the client and his or her needs and to be able to assess the way in which the helping relationship is developing. Helpers who are not able to display this confidence in their own skills will rarely be successful in helping others.

It is important that this quality of helping is seen to be more than a question of image management. Confidence in the helper's skills is about more than the display of credentials and qualifications on a wall: it is about the person in need feeling sure that he or she is understood and that the helper is able to deal effectively with the concerns raised.

This issue of competence is not the same as that of the qualifications of the helper: a person can be qualified but not competent and a person can be unqualified and competent. For example, many non-lawyers are able to give legal advice about house purchase simply because they have experienced the problems of house purchase at first hand. Equally, many of those who offer help and counselling to others are not qualified. The question of competence is one of confidence.

Clarity of contract

Just as those in need seek competence so too do they seek some clear definition of what the limits to helping are. For example, they wish to know:

- how long will the helping relationship last – is it for just one session or five or 10 or 30?
- how long will a particular helping session be – 10 minutes or 20 or 50 or two hours?
- under what conditions can the helper be contacted outside the agreed sessions, if at all?
- what are the specific purposes of the helping relationship and are these purposes clear to *both* parties?
- how confidential is the relationship – is it to be wholly confidential or will the helper provide some information to others?
- under what conditions might the helping relationship terminate, other than those of the agreed time limit?

These questions, and many others which those in need have about the nature of the helping relationship, need to be addressed honestly and openly by the helper. Of course, the extent to which they are important will vary from one helping relationship to another and will also vary according to the type of help being offered. But these specific issues are pertinent to many forms of helping.

One way in which counsellors and helpers ensure that both they and the person in need are clear about the nature of the helping relationship is to make an explicit 'contract'. For example, the helper might state the extent of their availability and the extent and nature of confidentiality and may clearly limit the focus of the helping. They may do so by saying: (a) our helping activity will be restricted to four confidential 35-minute sessions at 10 am each Tuesday; (b) in this time we will seek to reduce the extent to which you feel anxious about examinations (or whatever); and (c) we will decide at the end of the four sessions whether another session is needed to accomplish this task or whether there are other tasks that you think are important and for which I can be of help.

The word 'contract' is unfortunate because it implies for many a formality and degree of commitment which is severe, especially if their experience of contracts is entirely legal. Nonetheless, what is happening in the example just given is that the helper is making a firm arrangement with a person to seek to help them deal with a specific problem – their anxiety about examinations. The absence of such a contract might enable either the helper to exploit the person in need or the person in need to exploit the services of the helper. A contract is one way to ensure that both parties begin a helping relationship with some clarity about its purposes and its duration.

Ethical behaviour

Those seeking help expect their helpers to behave ethically. They do not expect to be used as human subjects for some experiment or to be abused as a person.

Each year in both Britain and the United States a number of professional helpers are prosecuted for unethical conduct. Typically these prosecutions relate to the sexual exploitation of clients or to breaches of professional rules of conduct. For example, one Californian counsellor was prosecuted for practising what he termed 'rage reduction therapy' – clients were strapped naked to a table and subjected to tickling and masturbation. Their anger and rage subsided over time, which was not surprising given that the rage reduction sessions lasted over five hours! The counsellor claimed that this method increased clients' tolerance to anger and distress, whilst the court held that these practices were an abuse of the client's dignity and the counsellor's professional status.

Whilst this is an extreme example of professional misconduct, the situation most commonly feared by those who seek help is the abuse of trust or the breaching of confidentiality. When a person seeks help, even if they are simply seeking some information or guidance, they do not expect that the trust they have placed in a helper will be abused. There are several ways in which this abuse can take place:

- the helper can make use of information provided for their own financial or social gain

- the helper can use the information provided by a person in need so as to belittle that person
- the helper can inform a third party that the person in need is seeking help and this may be damaging to that person
- the helper may distort what the person in need is doing during the helping relationship in such a way as to reduce the client's feeling of confidence in the person of the helper.

Imagine a female client who seeks help because she has difficulty in achieving sexual satisfaction from normal heterosexual relationships. An unscrupulous counsellor may use her sexual vulnerability as a vehicle for satisfying either their own sexual needs or those of another person. Alternatively, the client explains her situation to the helper who then systematically distorts what the client has said so that it 'fits' into their own belief systems about, say, marriage or family life. Both of these examples involve the helper abusing the trust which the person in need has placed in them.

By far the most commonly expressed concern of clients is with confidentiality. They are concerned that a helper will disclose the fact that they have sought help or that the helper will discuss the detail of what has passed between the client and themselves to another person. More often than not, their concern is that some disclosure will take place to a member of their family or to their employer. For example, a teenage girl was distressed to find that, whenever she had talked in confidence (so she thought) to a school counsellor her parents had been informed of the nature of her concerns. This girl felt that the counsellor had betrayed the trust of their relationship whilst at the same time becoming a part of her problem rather than a part of its solution.

Counsellors and helpers should make clear what the limits of their confidentiality are. They should indicate clearly to a person in need that the material they are disclosing could or must be told to a third party if this is the case. In making clear the limits to their confidentiality helpers should not assume that they will never breach the confidentiality that they offer. Counsellors and helpers, like doctors and priests, may need to disclose information to a court under certain circumstances. Though these are rare occasions, usually involving serious criminal or civil cases, the fact is that a judge can order a helper (including a doctor or a priest, but not a lawyer) to disclose what was said during a consultation; they also have the power to require any notes or documents kept by the helper to be released to the court if it is felt that the material they contain would assist the court in its work. Judges exercise discretion and caution in requiring these legally sanctioned breaches of confidentiality, since they recognize that the very fabric of helping relationships is based upon confidentiality and trust. But where justice demands disclosure, according to Lord Denning (a former Master of the Rolls), disclosure has to be required by the courts.

These rare legal occasions aside, there are times when it is helpful to clients to breach the confidentiality of a helping relationship. For example, if you suspect that the person you have been seeing is likely to try and commit suicide then it may be advisable to ask close relatives or friends to keep a watchful eye out and to inform you of any unusual behaviour. In thinking about such cases you might like to consider this guideline offered to counsellors by the American Psychological Association (APA): 'Information received in confidence is revealed only after the most careful deliberation and when there is clear and imminent danger to an individual or to society, and then only to appropriate professional workers or public authorities.' A similar guideline offered by the American Personnel and Guidance Association (APGA) reads: 'When the client's condition indicates that there is clear and imminent danger to the client or others, the (helper) must take reasonable personal action to inform responsible authorities ... consultation with other professionals must be used where possible.' So helpers faced with a person who seems to be endangering themselves or others need to exercise sound judgement as to the extent and nature of the risk and the consequences of disclosing information to others. They also need to consider the way in which their client is to be informed about the breach of confidentiality and what support they can offer if the client feels unable to have confidence in the helper.

A great deal of time can be spent by helpers worrying about confidentiality and its implications. In practice, however, it is an issue that arises only rarely. Nor does it often assume the severity of consequences briefly discussed here. Counselling and helping organizations need a clear view about the nature of confidentiality and individual helpers need to consider the ethics of breaching a person's confidence. But an over-emphasis on confidentiality in the abstract is likely to produce a confused response on those rare occasions when it is a real and pressing concern.

Realistic expectations

Many of those who seek help have unrealistic expectations of what can be achieved in a limited number of sessions. For example, one young man I saw who was extremely depressed and had been for over a year was hopeful that in four or five sessions I could remove his depression and give him back 'some enjoyment in life'. Many of those who seek educational responses to their needs at the Open University are very disappointed when they realize that their needs cannot be met in a year – it may take between four and eight years to obtain the qualification they are seeking. Those seeking help can have unreal expectations about both *what* can be achieved and *the time* it can take to achieve it.

Many of those who seek the help of counsellors or voluntary workers in helping organizations utilize what is known as 'the medical model' of helping. They assume that, once they have described what is happening to them (described the *symptoms*), the helper will understand (*diagnose*) their problem (*illness*) and give advice (*offer a cure*) which will lead them to resolve their problem (*get better*) and function normally. They expect their helper to undertake most of the work. But the reality should be that it is the person in need that does most of the work. The medical model is not the predominant model being applied.

This feature of helping – that those seeking help also have a model of helping (the medical model) which is not an appropriate description of a great deal that takes place in the name of helping – creates further problems for the person seeking help and their helper. This discrepancy between what the person expects and what actually happens often leads some to feel that they are not getting the 'right kind' of help; or that their helper is ineffective, since he or she is not telling them what to do; or that they are making slow progress, and they had hoped for more after so many sessions.

Those seeking help often have unrealistic expectations of what a helper can do and are frequently unhappy with the early phase of helping. To counteract this tendency, helpers need to ensure that their contracting with those they are helping is explicit enough to cover the practical issues already mentioned and is also offering some guidance about the style of helping that is being offered. Realistic goal setting, explicit statements about styles of working, and discussion of the responsibilities of the person seeking help are all essential ingredients of the contracting process. A failure to undertake these tasks will lead, in some cases, to early termination of the helping relationship and in others to frustration and a lack of commitment to the helping relationship on the part of the person in need.

Styles of working

Just as it is sometimes necessary to match the gender and social background of the person in need so style of working of the helper needs to be matched to the style of working of the person in need.

The term 'style of working' refers to the forms of helping described in Chapter 1. These forms of helping become guidelines for the way in which the helper interacts with the person in need. For example, one style focuses upon emotional dischage (cathartic), whilst another is more directive and informative. These descriptions of the forms of helping are just one feature of the *style of the helper*. There are two more. One concerns the extent to which different features of the person are the focus of attention. For example, some helpers work largely with *thinking* processes – with information, patterns of thought, irrational thoughts, self-talk; others work largely with *behaviour* – with the mannerisms a person has, with the performance of some social skill, seeking to reduce the incidence of some undesirable behaviour; yet others concentrate on *feelings* and *emotions* – encouraging the person to express emotions and experience them, with emotional discharge and with activities which are intended to focus the person's attention on the way in which they experience emotion towards other people. The focus of a helper upon one or more of these three different features is also a part of the helper's style. The final feature of style which I mention here is the extent to which the helper is *confronting* when working with a person. Some helpers are more confronting than others and seek to push the person hard to learn about themselves, or to seek the right information, or to explore their feelings or change their behaviour. Others are less confronting and demanding.

The description of style, then, involves three elements:

- the forms of helping a person engages in
- the focus for helping – that is, the emphasis the helper gives to thinking, feeling and/or behaviour
- the extent to which the helper is confronting and demanding of those they are seeking to help.

Research studies show clearly that the helper's style needs to be matched to the style expectations of the client if the helping is to be maximally effective. However, such studies presuppose that both the helper and the person seeking help have a clear understanding of what they expect and how they normally interact. It also presupposes that the person in need has a choice about where to obtain help from – something that is not always possible, especially in rural communities. Nonetheless, the fact remains that compatibility of working styles is an ingredient in the success of helping relationships.

Forms of helping

Whilst many of the comments made in this chapter may seem to relate to the facilitative forms of helping more than to the directive forms of helping (see Chapter 2), it is in fact the case that several of the issues raised are pertinent to all forms of helping. For example, the ethical issues apply just as much to informative helping as to cathartic helping; comments about styles of working and about gender and social background matching are also pertinent. Each helper needs to review the materials in this chapter and examine their own work in the light of the points raised. There is a summary of all the points to consider at the end of the chapter.

Manipulation

There are several forms of manipulation which those seeking help sometimes use. The simplest way of describing these manipulations is to see them as 'games' which people use in order to achieve some purpose. The commonest game is 'I am right, aren't I?' (sometimes seen as 'take my side'), in which the person in need seeks to use the helper to bolster their position. This is seen frequently in marital counselling where one partner will ask the helper to confirm that the other is being unreasonable. Another of these manipulation games is 'tell me just how bad my condition is', in which the person seeks the helper's confirmation that their situation is hopeless and therefore it is alright for them to experience depression or anxiety or fear or whatever. This is commonly encountered by those helpers who counsel students about examination fears. A third game is 'this is getting us nowhere' which, if untrue, is a common defence *against* change.

There are a great many such games which helpers can readily identify. They have in common the fact that the person seeking help is either seeking confirmation for their current state or seeking to resist change. They constitute a manipulation in the sense that the person in need is seeking to prevent the helper changing their conception of themselves, their problem or both, and they are seeking to prevent the helper pushing them to change.

Such manipulations occur readily when the contracts between the helper and those they seek to help are unclear, when ethical boundaries have been crossed or when there is a mismatch between the working style of the helper and that of the person seeking help. Manipulations are not necessarily unhealthy – they can provide the helper with valuable materials which help confront the person and contribute positively to the helping process – but they have first to be detected by the helper. The problem with manipulation is that it is such a part of the helping process that the helper needs to be able to stand back from the helping relationship in order to be able to detect the fact that manipulation is taking place. A failure to detect a manipulation can lead the helper and the person they are seeking to help down a blind alley and make the helping grossly ineffective.

Conclusion

I have examined some of the ways in which helpers perceive those who help them. Ethical questions and questions about helper–client compatibility have also been addressed. The overall conclusion you might reach from reading this chapter is the need to make explicit the assumptions you are making as a helper about the nature of the helping relationship you see to be appropriate for the particular person you are helping.

In making your assumptions explicit, the following checklist of points may be useful to you.

• Does the client feel that they need to be helped by a person of the same sex?
• Does the client feel that your social background in any way inhibits your ability to help?
• What can you tell the client that will help them have confidence in you?
• What do you need to do in order to retain the client's confidence in you?
• How long do you think the helping relationship will last?
• What will be the duration in time of the sessions?
• What will be the expectations you have of the person in need during these sessions? Are there any specific preparations you expect from the client?
• What is your style of working and how will this be experienced by the person in need?
• What ethical statements do you wish to make at the beginning of the relationship – for example, about confidentiality?
• What rights does the person in need have during the time they are

with you? (This is essentially a question about styles of working – who is in control of the session and under what circumstances might this control change?)

- What are the specific purposes of the helping relationship – are these understood by the helper and the person in need?
- Under what conditions will or can the relationship be terminated and by whom?
- Under what conditions can the person in need contact the helper outside agreed session times (if at all)?

This checklist should help you think about the nature of the contract you have with the person you are helping and sensitize you to some of the issues which need to be addressed early in any helping relationship that is intended to last for two or more sessions. It is explicitly *not* intended to be a checklist that is used during a session with a person in need as if it were a quiz which both of you needed to answer.

This last point emphasizes a point made repeatedly in the previous two chapters. Counselling and helping are particular forms of relationship between people. As such they are not governed by strict rules of conduct or proforma questionnaires. Rather they are dynamic and mutual – the outcome of the helping process is the product of the quality of this relationship. During such a relationship both the helper and the person in need may be required to take risks – to offer interpretation, information or suggestions which the other might find threatening. The person seeking help may feel anxious or confronted; they may feel insecure yet confident that some progress towards their specific goal is being achieved. What matters most is that the helper is able to be sensitive to their immediate needs whilst at the same time being aware of the long-term effects of what is happening between them.

Part 2. The People Element

Chapter 4

Helping the Individual Cope

A considerable amount of the time of a counsellor or helper is given
to helping a person cope better with some stress or concern. The person in need approaches the helper with comments such as: 'I just
don't know what to do next ...', or 'I have tried everything, but nothing seems to work ...', or 'I can't stand any more of ...'. All of these
statements are indications that the person currently feels unable to
cope.

There are three ways in which helpers find themselves working
with people in need in terms of coping. These are:

- to help people learn new coping skills – for example, through
training in assertiveness or social skills
- reinforcing existing coping skills and showing their relevance
to current events – for example, by encouragement or by providing new information which activates the person's own coping
repertoire
- restoring the person's ability to cope after coping has failed,
perhaps because of a crisis of some kind.

A counsellor or helper can act to promote coping in each of these
three ways. I now examine in particular the ways in which coping
can be restored following a crisis.

The nature of coping

In common speech coping is referred to as an outcome of some
activity. People think of themselves as having coped either well or
badly with some event. Others examine the behaviour of a friend
under stress and say 'She coped well with that ...' or 'He coped
badly with the stress of all that ...', whatever 'that' might have been.

Psychologists, however, do not see coping in this way. Psychologists think of coping as a *process*. Richard Lazarus, a psychologist specializing in stress and coping research at the University of California, suggests that coping is not a single act but a series of activities which the person uses when faced with stressors of various kinds. When a person uses a tactic from within a coping strategy – for example, seeking to change the situation by achieving a consensus – then they also affect the situation itself. A change in the situation of this kind may then require a new and different coping tactic, and so the process continues. Coping is thus a part of the process of interacting with the social environment rather than an outcome of such an interaction.

Let me illustrate this point with a number of examples from different settings.

> Jean is a final year student at a college of further education and she is near to sitting her examinations. Mike is in the same position. Jean prepares herself carefully for the exam, checks previous exam papers, practises writing her answers under exam conditions, gets other students and friends to test her on her knowledge. She seeks to solve the problem of doing examinations by rehearsal and the use of social support. In contrast, Mike uses a wishful thinking coping tactic. He wishes that he knew the answers to the questions that might come up and does some work, but not much, in preparation for the exam. He is outwardly expressing confidence about his chances, but is inwardly worried that he will fail.

In this example we notice two different coping strategies – logical problem-solving and denial. These strategies are pursued by different tactics. Jean uses rehearsal and the seeking out of social support as a way of logically dealing with the problem of having to sit an examination; Mike uses wishful thinking and social camouflage (that is, having one message for his friends and a different one for himself) as tactics in his denial. The same situation – having to sit an examination – produces two very different coping responses.

Now consider the following situation:

> Gill has to have an operation to remove a diseased portion of her lung, as does Sylvia. Gill copes with the stress of impending surgery by ignoring all the information her doctors provide about the nature of the disease and about the effects of the surgery and simply submits herself to the surgical process. Sylvia,

on the other hand, seeks out information about her condition and reads some literature about it; she asks a great many questions about the surgery since she seeks to have a clear picture of what the surgery will mean in terms of post-operative discomfort, pain and mobility. Following the operation Sylvia reports only minor pain and is up and about quite quickly – the post-operative experience is very much as she anticipated. Gill, however, is in considerable pain and finds that she is hardly able to move during the first three days. In fact Sylvia is discharged after four days and Gill is discharged after eight.

It is not being suggested in this case that Gill took longer to recover from surgery simply because of the effects of her coping strategy, though there is growing evidence that certain coping strategies do lead to earlier recovery from surgery and that these strategies can be actively promoted by doctors and nurses in the pre and post-operative periods. What is being said here is that Gill's coping differs significantly from the coping strategy adopted by Sylvia and that Gill's coping strategy contributes to her longer stay in hospital.

These two situations – the examination and impending surgery – illustrate two things. First, people adopt different coping strategies when faced with events which they regard as stressful. Second, these different strategies contribute in different ways to the experience of stress – that is, the coping strategy adopted is a part of the experience of stress, not something apart fom it.

This last point will become clear when the next example is considered.

Dave and Mike have both been recently divorced. Both had been married for six years and both had children who are now in the care of their former wives. Dave sees divorce as a release from a difficult situation: he and his wife had spent the last two years of their married life arguing, being depressed (both had seen psychiatrists) and being unfaithful. Neither Dave nor his wife found marriage to be satisfactory during these years and for their own sakes as well as for the sake of their son they agreed on a divorce. Mike's experience is very similar, though the difference is an important one: Mike outwardly agreed to a divorce but inwardly experienced this as a failure rather than a release. Dave is living in a flat and copes with the experience of divorce by treating it as a problem to which he and his former wife found a rational and logical solution; Mike copes with the experience of failure by drinking and taking drugs. So serious has Mike's drinking and drug-taking become that the courts have recently refused him access to his former wife and to his child. This development confirms Mike's feelings of failure and leads him to drink more.

In this example we see something about coping that is important for helpers to fully understand: the coping strategy or tactic a person adopts can be a *part* of their problem rather than a part of the solution to their problem. For example, Mike's coping strategy is essentially a denial strategy (he is denying his own feelings of failure) which is expressed through his tactic of drinking and drug-taking. Whilst this tactic enables Mike to deny his inner feelings to some extent, it also makes his social situation worse and acts to confirm his inner feeling. What started out as a strategy for overcoming his feelings of failure ends up reinforcing this feeling.

This feature of coping – the fact that a coping strategy or tactic can contribute to making a situation more stressful rather than less – is seen frequently through the use of what is termed 'displacement coping'. It occurs when a person seeks to deal with their anger or frustration about work by expressing anger or frustration at home; alternatively, it occurs when a person brings their domestic problems into work in such a way that their ability to work is impaired by their domestic difficulties.

Three major coping strategies

Two American psychologists, Leonard Pearlin and Carmi Schooler, surveyed 2,300 adults aged between 18 and 65 in Chicago and examined the ways in which they said they had coped with some recent stressful experiences. In analysing this information they were concerned to identify the major strategies for coping which people actually used when faced with real-life events. They identified three major coping strategies which are relevant at this point in our examination of the nature of coping.

Faced with major life-events (such as the death of a spouse, the loss of a job or becoming a parent for the first time), those surveyed in Chicago used one or more of three major strategies. These were:

1. *Seeking to change their situation in such a way as to solve their problem.* Examples of the tactics used in this strategy include:
   • looking for a compromise between their own needs and those of others
   • talking out their situation with those most involved in it

• adding a new feature to the situation so as to provide new personal resources which will aid the coping process.

2. *Redefining the meaning of a stressful situation after it has occurred.* Examples of the tactics used in this strategy include:
   • rationalizing the experience – saying to oneself '... it could have been much worse', or 'worse has happened to me before ...'
   • turning a negative experience into a positive one – 'though I hated it at the time, I did learn a lot about myself ...', or 'these things are sent so that we can learn'
   • positive comparison with others – 'I felt I wasn't doing too well until I looked at how Fred was doing'.

3. *Controlling the stress as an experience when it happens.* Typical tactics adopted under this strategy include:
   • relax and calm down – things will get better when I feel in control
   • positive connotation – 'there must be something positive in this situation which I'm missing right now, so I'll search for it'
   • time will heal – 'this feels bad right now, but I know from experience that it will look different in a few days' time'.

These statements about coping strategies are helpful to those acting as counsellors and helpers, since they provide a framework for understanding the coping experience of the person in need. Helpers can use these strategy descriptions to encourage the person in need to identify their own approach to their stress problems.

Pearlin and Schooler, in looking at their Chicago data, examined the question 'Are some of these strategies more effective than others in dealing with stressful life events?'. Their answer is interesting. They suggest that the most effective coping persons – those that find few situations stressful or threatening – are those who are able to move between these three strategies with ease and who have a variety of coping tactics available to them. Developing this work further, members of the Chicago stress project team noted that those who were regarded as the most 'hardy' (that is, the most effective in coping with stressful life events) had three salient features: (a) they felt that they were very much in control of their own lives; (b) they enjoyed and sought out challenges; and (c) they had a strong commitment to self-survival. These three features coupled with a broad coping repertoire enable people to cope with difficult situations. The absence of these features is likely to lead to stressful experiences and, in certain circumstances, crisis.

Clearly, not all of those who present themselves as in need of help can describe themselves as 'hardy', though helpers should recognize that some of those seeking help are hardy and seek help so as to confirm their own successful coping activities. The helper's task is most frequently to restore a minimum level of coping which is appropriate to the person's current experience.

Coping tactics and processes

When faced with some stressful situation, such as a major domestic argument, a pending forced retirement or being made unemployed, what does a person do? Richard Lazarus, already mentioned in this chapter, suggests that there are two stages in our responses. The first is to ask the question 'Am I OK or am I in trouble?'. The second stage involves us in asking the question '... and can I cope?'

The first of these stages, which Lazarus calls the primary appraisal stage, involves a number of different considerations. For example, the person is asking questions such as 'Is this situation relevant or irrelevant to me?'; they are exploring the question 'Is this a challenge to which I can respond, or a threat?'; and they are asking 'To what extent can I benefit from this situation, or is it the case that no matter what I try to do I will lose out?'. All of the questions asked at this primary appraisal stage involve the person in relating current events to their beliefs, the way in which they see themselves (what psychologists call the self-concept), to the goals which they regard as important for themselves and to the level of their current commitments. Thus, primary appraisal is a statement not only about the situation in which people find themselves but about themselves.

Given this observation about the nature of primary appraisal – that it is concerned with the way in which people see themselves in relation to a given situation – then it should be clear to the helper that they will often need to explore the assumptions which the person makes at this level. For example, a person who has a poor view of their own worth and abilities may regard some situation as 'hopeless' when in fact a few small actions could render that same situation beneficial. Just because this person's primary appraisal is negative it does not follow that the situation is threatening or hopeless; it may equally be the case that the person is regarding themselves as hopeless.

The second stage that Lazarus refers to (he regards it as a secondary appraisal) is the nature of the person's coping repertoire. On the basis of their primary appraisal, their past experience, the strength of their own self-confidence and material resources the person asks 'What is in my coping repertoire that will help me deal with this situation?'. This repertoire may be extensive or small and, as we have seen, the more extensive the repertoire the more likely it is that the person will be able to call upon an appropriate coping response.

At the secondary appraisal stage, a coping failure may imply one of several difficulties. The first is the lack of an appropriate coping response in the person's coping repertoire. The second is a lack of previous experience of having to cope with such a situation – a problem encountered frequently by those facing up to the loss of a close relative or friend for the first time. In this latter case, the person may have a clear idea of what to do (intellectual coping knowledge) but lack the experience to put that knowledge into use. A third reason for a coping failure may be the person's lack of material resources (that is, cash, mobility, social contacts and social support) to put a particular coping tactic into action. The helper needs to discern which of these three situations provides the best hypothesis for the failure of a person to cope with a situation which they have correctly regarded as threatening.

The experience of coping failure

When a person is totally unable to cope with some situation then that person is said to be in crisis. My colleague Ray Woolfe and I have characterized a crisis thus:

- symptoms of stress – the person experiences stress physically or psychologically or both
- attitude of panic or defeat – because the person feels that they have exhausted their coping repertoire, they feel helpless and are often overwhelmed by feelings of inadequacy or pointlessness
- focus on relief – the person seeks relief from the feeling of being in a crisis rather than a solution to their problem
- lowered efficiency – in areas of life other than those directly associated with the crisis the person may appear to be functioning normally, but with reduced efficiency
- limited duration – because the experience of crisis is psychologically painful, it does not last for long and can be regarded as an acute experience of limited duration.

I elaborated on this technical description in a study of crisis in marriage. The experience of crisis was as follows:

1. *The way people see themselves:*
   They feel that their self-esteem is threatened.
   They lack confidence in themselves.
   They deprecate their own abilities.
   They question their self-worth.
   They defend idealized versions of their own behaviour.

2. *The way people experience the world:*
   They find reality both complex and overwhelming.
   They see their position in the world as determined by people other than themselves.
   They experience the world as a place in which they have to use tactics like denial, wishful thinking or helplessness in order to survive, even though they can recognize some of the implications of such tactics.

3. *The way they experience their own emotional world:*
   Anxiety and feelings of panic predominate.
   They feel helpless and overwhelmed.
   They feel indifferent.
   They cannot accept praise or compliments.

4. *The way in which they think:*
   Their thinking is disorganized.
   They feel unable to make decisions or to take responsibility for their actions.
   They lack the ability to 'stand outside their situation' and review their predicament with any objectivity.
   They are resistant to change.

5. *Their physical state:*
   They do not attend to their physical needs.
   There is a loss of appetite.
   Sleep patterns are disturbed.
   In extreme cases, some psychosomatic illness may occur – for example, muscular tension, gout, ulcers.
   Prolonged experience of crisis can exacerbate existing symptoms – including heart disease and cancer.

Not all those in crisis will experience all these features. The extent to which they do will depend upon their previous experience of similar situations, their coping repertoire and the extent to which their primary appraisal made them feel threatened or under pressure. Nonetheless, many of these features will be present during a crisis.

Helping tasks

Faced with these kinds of experience and a time-urgent problem, what is the counsellor or helper to do? How can the helper react to a crisis situation in a way which does not add to the problems which the person in crisis is already experiencing?

Several counsellors have suggested that there is a model of helping which is very appropriate when the helper is seeking simply to restore the ability of a person to cope with their own problems in their own way. This model has been elaborated by Schwartz. He says that there are seven steps the helper needs to take. These are:

1. *Help the person face up to the crisis.*
Discourage denial and promote some objectivity in their thinking about the current situation. Make sure that they are accurate in their primary appraisal. Look at the extent to which the crisis is shaped by their own actions and thoughts.

2. *Break up the crisis into manageable doses.*
To prevent the person from being overwhelmed by the situation encourage them to see their actions as a series of steps which they need to take and ensure that these steps are manageable and discrete.

3. *Stop them guessing and promote objectivity and accurate secondary appraisal.*
The person in crisis has a poor grasp of reality. Encourage the use of objective data and rational thinking – get them to stop thinking emotionally and irrationally. Get them to evaluate their own performance as a coping person and encourage objectivity about this feature of their behaviour.

4. *Avoid false reassurance.*
Just as helpers seek to promote objectivity in the person they are seeking to help, so they should be objective in their own evaluations of that person's progress and prospects. The helper must avoid being over-optimistic and confident about the ability of a person in crisis to take command of their own situation.

5. *Discourage projection.*
The term 'projection' has not yet been mentioned in this chapter. It refers to the attribution of certain qualities (for example, guilt, anger, aggression, jealousy or fear) by one person to another when in fact these qualities are more present in the person doing the attribution than they are in the person receiving the attribution.

Put simply, projectors accuse others of doing to them what they are doing to others. When a person is in crisis, projection is common and tends to make personal relationships difficult. Helpers have a major task to discourage projection.

6. *Help and encourage individuals to help themselves, especially by connecting them to their own network of social supports.*
The individual in crisis will seek dependence on their helper unless clear steps are taken by that helper to 'make the person work for themselves'. The helper needs to encourage the person to make personal decisions, to work with others, to seek support from others in the work that they have to do in order to overcome the crisis. They must be enabled and encouraged to become active rather than passive, connected to others rather than estranged, and in control of their own actions rather than dependent.

7. *The helper needs to teach active coping skills.*
When someone first presents in crisis it is likely that either normal coping responses have become ineffective or that the normal coping responses are inappropriate for the situation. The helper has to do more than just understand the problem which the person is faced with: they have to teach new ways of coping which are both appropriate and likely to be effective. The helper has to be active and not simply a listener.

These seven steps need to be seen in the context of the helping processes outlined in the first part of this book. That is, the helper needs to establish a rapport and commitment on the part of the person in need through the use of empathy, warmth and genuineness and needs to have a clear contract for working with the person. A failure to establish a helping relationship which has a boundary agreed through a contract will make helping a person in crisis difficult.

We can summarize the tasks of the helper working with people in crisis under the same headings as were used to describe the experience of crisis.

The way people see themselves:
- re-establish a sense of self-worth
- stop self-deprecation and promote a positive view of self
- turn negative defences into positive prescriptions for action.

The way people experience the world:
- promote objectivity in thinking about their situation

- ensure that they take responsibility for their own part in the creation of the problem
- increase their feeling of control (or mastery) of the situation in which they find themselves
- encourage them to think of the present and future more than the past and present
- discourage wishful thinking and encourage rationality
- teach coping skills where appropriate
- discourage dependence.

The way they experience their emotional world:
- encourage them to identify more accurately their own emotional experiences
- discourage projection
- reduce the level of anxiety
- encourage the acceptance of positive feelings.

The way in which they think:
- encourage purposive thinking
- break up the crisis into manageable doses
- focus upon specific goals
- restore the ability to 'stand outside' themselves and review their situation
- enable them to envisage the prospect of change.

Their physical state:
- seek to ensure that they eat regularly
- seek to ensure that they sleep adequately
- the helper should seek to ensure that their physical well-being is as important to the person as is their material and psychological well-being.

These lists of tasks provided by both Schwartz and myself suggest that helping a person in crisis is demanding work. It is. Furthermore, it is work that is generally pressured by the time-urgency of the situation. The tasks listed here constitute the 'ideal' of crisis counselling and helping – in practice, helpers will find themselves using these task listings as reminders of the possibilities rather than as specific agendas for action with every person they see. Nonetheless, these lists provide a reminder to helpers of the substantive nature of helping tasks for a person facing a crisis.

Teaching coping skills

So far I have been concerned with the promotion of coping for those for whom coping is needed urgently. The helping tasks outlined are also appropriate for restoring coping to those who find themselves *temporarily* bereft of coping skills. But there is a further area of work that helpers are increasingly involved with: the development of coping skills for those who are not in crisis or under stress but who wish to increase their coping skills repertoire. Known as 'coping skills training' or 'social skills training' (and sometimes as psycho-education), this area of work more closely resembles teaching and coaching than counselling or psychotherapy, but has become increasingly important in preparing people for events which are likely to happen to them.

The next chapter deals in detail with this form of helping activity. What is relevant here is the extent to which the helper's tasks in promoting active coping during a crisis are relevant to the teaching of coping skills in non-crisis situations.

The teaching of coping skills – what one psychologist has referred to recently as 'personal effectiveness training' – now embraces a great many skill areas. These include:

- planning and decision-making skills
- skills of being assertive rather than aggressive
- communication skills to enhance the quality of relationships
- skills for specific life-events, such as marriage, becoming a parent, dealing with job interviews, coping with bereavement and coping with terminal illness.

In each of these forms of skills training the training programme is similar. The helper assesses the current skill levels of the person in need, breaks down the skills to be mastered into manageable units of work, rehearses the person (through role-play and practice sessions) in the new skills, sets tasks to be completed in the 'real world' which involve the use of the new skills, and helps the person evaluate their performance. All this is undertaken within the confines of an agreed programme of work (equivalent to a contract) and the person in need is encouraged to assume an increasing responsibility for learning coping skills. Throughout, the aim is to encourage the person to increase the repertoire of appropriate and effective coping and to know that these coping skills can be used in a variety of situations.

Coping skills training, which is elaborated in the next chapter, has close parallels with the description of crisis work outlined earlier. There are, however, two important differences. The need to develop skills is more urgent in crisis work than in coping skills training –

the helper will therefore find him or herself being much more directive when dealing with a person in crisis as the period of training
is much shorter. Secondly, the person undertaking skills training
has several opportunities to make errors both in the rehearsal and
practice of the skills during training sessions and in the use of the
skills in 'safe' real-life tasks. In contrast, the person in crisis usually
has little margin for error in the use of skills promoted during counselling and helping sessions. Though these differences are significant, there is a clear parallel between these two kinds of helping
activity.

Given these parallels it is possible to suggest that helpers are often
called upon to act as teachers or coaches for a person or a group who
have specific needs. This teaching role is just as much a part of helping and counselling as others to be examined later. What is important is that the role is undertaken with a clear understanding of the
processes involved.

Suggested reading

Murgatroyd, S. and Woolfe, R. (1982) *Coping with Crisis – Understanding and
Helping Persons in Need*. London: Harper and Row.
An introduction to the idea of coping in the context of both developmental and unexpected crisis situations. It includes materials on death, unemployment, divorce,
parenting, rape, and growing old. A standard text in many social work and counselling training programmes, but not difficult to read.

Murgatroyd, S. and Woolfe, R. (1985) *Helping Families in Distress – An
Introduction to Family Focussed Helping*. London: Harper and Row.
This book, which contains a great deal of case material, examines the ways in which
individual distress is produced within families. It examines several different ways
helpers can affect individual distress through family-focused work.

Meichenbaum, D. (1983) *Coping with Stress*. London: Century Publishing.
An excellent introduction to the social and psychological nature of stress and ways
of coping. Illustrated with case materials and cartoons, this book is not difficult to
read and contains many practical suggestions for coping skills development. Highly
recommended.

Chapter 5

Helping and Social Skills

Social Skills Training (SST) has been practised under a variety of different names. These include Life Skills Training, Personal Effectiveness Training (and its offshoots – Parent Effectiveness Training, Leadership Effectiveness Training and Teacher Effectiveness Training), Structured Learning Therapy and Coping Skills Training. All these forms of helping are, essentially, different ways of teaching social skills. They differ from each other in the way that the process of helping through teaching is understood.

SST is best thought of as being *directive* rather than *facilitative*. It is essentially an informative form of helping – helpers assess and evaluate the skills of the person, provide coaching and instruction intended to develop new skills or refine existing ones, help the person practise these 'new' skills and provide feedback and support to them in their use of the skills. In addition, this form of helping often (though not always) focuses upon *behaviour* rather than *thoughts* or *feelings*. Whilst some of the SST programmes to be examined here focus upon both behaviour and thoughts as the prime targets for change, many communications skills programmes focus upon behaviour. This last observation is important in that it directs the attention of the helper to some behavioural ways of promoting skills development.

Three kinds of SST

In their discussion of different types of SST, Roger Ellis and Dorothy Whittington suggest that there are three kinds of SST.

Remedial SST – where the aim of the SST helper is to enable the person in need to develop and extend their repertoire of social behaviours. Their existing social skills are deemed by themselves or others to be inadequate for everyday life.

Developmental SST – where the helper aims to accelerate and facilitate the use of social skills in appropriate situations because the person in need currently uses them ineffectively or inappropriately. The aim is to make the use of existing skills more precise and more effective.

Specialized SST – where the helper aims to promote high levels of skill for those who need them in connection with their work – it is essentially a form of professional development.

Here are examples of SST under each of these three categories. Examples of *remedial SST* include training in basic communication skills for long-stay psychiatric patients about to return into the community or training in aggression management; preparation for job interviews or for marriage have both seen as examples of *developmental SST*; and training for counselling and health visiting have both been used as case studies of *specialized SST*.

The three levels described here are associated with the way in which the helper and trainee view the trainee's needs and circumstances. There is also an implicit assumption about the level of generality of the skills to be promoted through SST programmes. In the first two types of SST the levels of skill are often generalized – they involve skills which are applicable to a great many situations. In the third type of SST the skill level is usually specific – it is concerned with the particular form of social interaction associated with a particular occupational group.

These three types of SST can be practised either individually or in groups. The decision to help someone develop SST individually is usually taken by the helper, primarily in the light of their assessment of the skill needs of the person. A related consideration is the helper's judgement about the likely impact of this. Since a prime concern of the helper is to provide a safe environment for the practice of skills and for evaluation, the helper should be cautious about recommending group-based SST, even though this is likely to be beneficial to most participants.

Styles of SST training

Behavioural SST is the most frequently reported and evaluated style. The helper begins the evaluation of need by scrutinizing the actual behaviour of the person. Though they might listen to the person's explanations of their behaviour, they are most interested in the behaviour itself. Thus if a person says 'I always blush when I am introduced to new people, because I am worried about what they will think of me', the behaviourist SST helper notes the observed behaviour (blushing) and pays little attention to the person's own unobservable explanation for their behaviour (concern about self–other evaluation). The aim of the helper in this case would be to reduce the incidence of blushing. They would seek to affect this observable behaviour by a careful scrutiny of all other behaviours that precede the blush and are consequent upon it. They would seek to understand how this particular piece of behaviour has been learned and develop a way of promoting new learning which did not involve blushing. What the helper is most likely to do in these circumstances is to change the rewards the person associates with the act of meeting a new person. Rather than having to use a blush in order to 'cover up' their anxiety, the helper would seek to encourage the person to associate meeting a new person with a behavioural response that would benefit them in some way.

Most assertiveness training programmes use a behavioural approach. The person seeking to become more assertive is encouraged to practise phrases and techniques of interacting which place them on an equal footing with those they are seeking to be assertive with. Thus the person is encouraged to say what they are thinking in a way that strengthens their right to express their own opinions, without belittling the other person. This behavioural shaping by the helper concentrates upon observable behaviour (the statements the person makes) rather than their feelings about this behaviour.

Behavioural approaches to SST have been effective in reducing alcohol consumption amongst hospitalized alcoholic patients and disturbed problem drinkers. Also, the quality of social interaction of patients with severe psychiatric disturbance (chronic psychotic patients) can improve as a result of behavioural SST. SST has had a notable failure, however, in the attempt to use it to reduce the smoking behaviour of 'heavy' (40-plus cigarettes a day) smokers. There are several studies reporting the success of the behavioural approach to assertiveness training.

Systems SST. A second style of SST is known as the 'systems approach' or the 'cybernetic approach'. Unlike the previous styles, this style gives emphasis to the person's own thoughts about their skills. People are encouraged to look at and collect evidence about their behaviour but are then encouraged to evaluate the way in which they process this information about themselves and to modify their thinking about that behaviour. For example, someone who deals with a critical comment about work by getting upset is encouraged to look at the behaviour he or she and the person offering the criticism have engaged in. The following kinds of questions are asked by the helper to trainees: 'Is it reasonable to expect this person, given their position, to offer comment and criticism about your work?'; 'Was the criticism offered in a way that was intended to threaten you?'. The helper then seeks to encourage trainees to reconsider their thinking about the behaviour they have encountered so that they are able to respond to such behaviour differently when it occurs subsequently.

There are clear links between the systems approach and the discussion of coping in the previous chapter. You will recall that Richard Lazarus suggested that a person engages in a primary and secondary appraisal of social situations. The primary appraisal involves asking the question 'Is this situation a challenge or a threat?'; secondary appraisal involves the question '... and can I cope?'. This style of SST seeks to modify the primary and secondary appraisals of those in need of SST.

Experiential SST. In this style, the helper makes the assumption that each trainee is unique, with unique skills and needs. The helper seeks to encourage the person to define personal skills and needs and facilitates the acting out and rehearsal of the skills through drama activities, role-play and dreamwork. The helper seeks to push the person as much as they can to recognize their own assumptions, values, beliefs and behaviours and confronts them in a way that is intended to offer support to the development of skills. Here is an example.

Cindy is unable to enjoy shopping. So strong is her distaste for shopping that she feels herself getting anxious when making out lists of the things she wants to buy. Whenever she shops, she finds herself being unpleasant to shop assistants and unclear about the requests she makes of them about goods and services. Her helper asks her to imagine the worst possible shopping situation she can and to enact that worst situation as a form of role-play. The helper contributes by suggesting more things that could happen to the point at which Cindy feels unable to continue. The helper then encourages Cindy to work at another drama in which she role-plays her normal shopping behaviour – behaviour which is far less traumatic than the 'worst possible' scenario she has just experienced. Throughout this second drama, the helper points out just how 'easy' this all is in comparison to the situation she has just played and compliments her on good performances. After playing these two drama roles, the helper discusses with Cindy ways of improving her shopping behaviour by changing the way she thinks about it – the helper tries to make the behaviour interesting, sets her challenges, sometimes accompanying her on shopping trips so that she can be reinforced for her work. The result is that Cindy is less anxious about shopping and can shop in less than half the time it used to take.

Though this procedure has a number of behavioural components, it is largely experiential – the helper's role is seen as one of drawing attention to Cindy's experience and encouraging her to confront its meaning. Describing and understanding the three styles of SST is important for those who wish to work as helpers, since the more explicit their understanding of these styles the more effective they are likely to be in the performance of the helping task. Helpers intending to work with SST should seek to master their own style of work and to fully understand its underlying assumptions.

The tasks of the helper in SST

The aims of the helper in SST are:

- To provide a safe (if demanding) opportunity for the person in need to develop and practise social skills.
- To build a helping relationship with the person in need such that they are able to give accurate feedback, confront and encourage the person to develop appropriate skills.
- To teach the person in need appropriate skills in such a way as to ensure that they will be used by the person in 'real life' (as opposed to simulated situations), where appropriate.

These three aims statements mask a tremendous amount of work. For example, the helper needs to assess the current level of skill of the person in need, and he or she needs to do this in a way that is both sensitive to the person's emotional frame of mind and yet is realistic and appropriate. Following an assessment, the helper needs to sensitize the person to their own level of skill and to encourage the person to see themselves as in need of skills training. Next they have to teach the person the appropriate skill, using techniques which match both the level of skill and also the person. They then

have to provide opportunities for the person to practise the skill
using such techniques as they think appropriate – for example, role-
playing, drama techniques, rehearsal of dialogue. Finally, they have
to provide feedback to the person about their practice performance
and set them tasks to complete in the world outside the helper's
room.

In a remedial skills programme aimed at enhancing interpersonal
communication and coping, Michael Argyle has developed eight
sets of activities appropriate to the needs of those seeking remedial
help. They are presented here as a hierarchy of increasing
complexity.

Observation skills
- getting information about a situation
- getting information about how others in that situation feel
about the situation
- clarifying the causes and nature of the behaviour of others
- self-observation
- recognition of emotions; recognition of attitudes
- differentiation between statements and action.

Listening skills
- reflection of feelings
- matching mood to that of others in the situation
- showing that you are paying attention by providing feedback
- verbal and non-verbal ways of communicating attention
- asking questions in a way that is supportive to others and
informative to self.

Speaking skills
- disclosure of factual information
- disclosure of feelings
- fluency of speech and non-verbal accompaniments of speech
- clarity in the expression of emotions and attitudes.

Meshing skills
- being able to mesh your points and ideas with those of others
- timing interventions in a way that shows recognition of others
- building on what others say and do.

Expression of attitudes
- how to express attitudes and beliefs in a way that is perceived
as non-aggressive by others
- matching the style of others or choosing a different style
deliberately so as to influence others.

Social routines
- greetings, farewells, making requests, gaining access to strangers
- offering compliments, praise, encouragement and congratulations
- showing and giving sympathy
- providing explanations in a non-humble way
- offering apologies
- saving face in an awkward situation
- being assertive without being aggressive.

Strategies and tactics
The person in need is expected to be able to understand the difference between strategies and tactics (see Chapter 1) and to be able to choose a strategy and appropriate tactics to perform during role-play and homework assignments. Typical strategies promoted at this stage are:
- rewarding others
- controlling others
- presenting self in the best possible light.

Situation training
The person is encouraged to act out in role-play situations in which they feel the skills will be useful so that the helper is able to provide feedback, advice and coaching to the person.

This remedial SST programme provides the framework for the helper to achieve the broad aims outlined here. It will be clear that such an SST programme involves the helper in a great deal of preparatory work and that he or she needs to be very sensitive to the emotional set of the person or group they are dealing with. Also clear from a detailed study of this particular SST programme is that it is *behaviourally* oriented – it is concerned primarily with affecting the behaviour of a person in need. As the level of skills the person needs to develop increases so the helper's task becomes more demanding and the training more complex.

Making SST relevant

SST programmes are not intended to be teaching programmes in which a body of skills is transferred from the helper to those in need. Rather, the programme has to be modified and *tailored* to match the individual needs of the person or the specific needs of a group. Specific needs determine the programme rather than the programme being fixed and immutable. The programme is modified and adapted so as to 'fit' the needs of those pursuing it.

Given this, helpers need to give thought to the following six points:

- The rationale of SST training programmes needs to be *clearly defined and explicit* so that the person in need understands the role the helper is taking and the tasks they are being asked to pursue – there is a need for a contract.

- Helpers who intend using video or audio as ways of giving feedback need to be mindful of the fact that such devices *pose threats* to those who are unused to them. Helpers therefore need to explain their usefulness and provide adequate opportunity for the person to get used to the equipment and the feedback process – the helper needs to promote a feeling of personal safety.

- Skills to be promoted should be *tailored* to both the current level of skill and typical situations for the person in need – the helper needs to ensure that the SST programme is personally significant and appropriate.

- Helpers need to take full account of *individual differences* in learning when working in groups and should design groupwork sessions in such a way as to encourage these individual differences to be expressed and worked with – helpers should design their SST groupwork around known individual differences.

- Practice sessions and role-play should *relate directly* to the life of the person – they should not involve situations which it is most unlikely that the person will experience. Helpers need to ensure that practice sessions and role-play are appropriate and relevant to the person in need.

- The helper should *provide feedback* to the person which fully reflects their individual skill level, intelligence and emotional state, and should also be aware of the level of emotional investment the person has made in the training and practice activities – the helper should remain sensitive to the person throughout the programme and most especially when they are giving feedback.

The helper needs to remember that SST does not take place in isolation from other events in the person's life and that the very nature of SST involves the person reflecting upon skills in their daily interactions. In designing SST programmes for particular individuals the helper needs to be mindful that the person brings to each meeting a set of relevant experiences and that they take away questions and possible behaviours with which they will experiment. The helper who chooses to work with SST will find it beneficial to take full account of these relevant experiences each time they meet the person or group with whom they are working.

An SST programme for anger control

Not all of the SST programmes that are currently described in the literature focus exclusively upon the behaviour of the person in need. Some, such as those developed in Canada, focus upon the relationship between the thoughts the person has about their situation and the behaviour they engage in. One such programme is the stress inoculation programme developed by Donald Meichenbaum. Its rationale is essentially that the person needs to be taught how to *think about their situation* in such a way that their thinking produces appropriate social behaviours.

The stress inoculation programme usually involves three stages. These stages can be accomplished in one session (an hour) or may take several sessions, depending upon the assessment the helper makes of the needs of the person.

- The helper develops a *clear understanding* of the way in which the person currently responds to stress – how they think and the behaviour that results from this way of thinking.
- The helper teaches *specific coping skills*, giving most emphasis to the thinking processes that accompany behaviour.
- The helper provides *graded practice* so that the person is able to use the new thinking pattern to produce appropriate behaviours.

As can be seen, these steps constitute the basic steps of SST programmes. The difference is that the stress inoculation programme looks closely at the things people *say to themselves* when they find themselves behaving in stressful situations. The person is encouraged to change this 'self-talk' so that their experience of stress is reduced and they can express their experience in a socially acceptable way.

Taking anger as a feature of the stress response of some people, the following self-talk statements are often used in this SST programme.

Preparing for anger. 'This could be difficult, but I know how to deal with it. I can work out a plan to deal with this. Stick to the issues – don't feel criticism as personal. You've been here before and have come out OK.'

Confronting anger. 'As long as I stay calm and don't let myself get excited I will be in control of this situation and myself. Concentrate on the positive and upon what has to be done. Don't jump to conclusions. They don't have to like you and you don't have to like them – but you have to work together whether they like you or not.'

Coping with feeling angry. 'I am getting tense – RELAX! Take a deep breath and give yourself a time to think. My feeling angry is a cue: I need a thinking-time. They want me to feel angry – so I won't. If I allow myself to be angry then I will make myself angry with me!'

Reflecting on the unresolved conflict. 'Thinking about it makes me upset – so I'll stop. Relax – it beats getting angry with yourself! The situation may seem hopeless – but it is not serious. Don't take it personally.'

Reflecting on a resolved conflict. 'I did good there – well done ... you deserve a treat! I could feel myself beginning to get upset, but it wasn't worth it. See, I CAN keep my cool!'

These self-talk statements are devices used to interrupt the normal flow of thoughts when anger is being experienced – if used appropriately, they should lead to the person changing their behaviour so that they can better cope with feelings of anger.

Similar self-talk SST programmes have been developed to deal with fear, anxiety, depression and other features of stress. Reference is made to some of these materials at the end of this chapter.

Assertiveness training

Like stress inoculation training, assertiveness training generally involves the helper in bringing to the attention of the person in need their own self-talk patterns and behaviour. In this context, assertiveness means the expression of one's own needs in a way that shows respect for the needs and rights of others. Assertiveness differs from aggression in the sense that the assertive person respects others, where the aggressive person shows disrespect for others.

Many of those who seek the help of others are lacking in assertiveness. Common situations include:

● feeling inhibited to reject advances or suggestions made by others
● feeling manipulated by others, but not knowing what to do
● feeling that there is a specific request to be made of another person, but lacking the confidence to make that request
● being frustrated at not being able to say things that you are thinking at the time that they need to be said

- finding it difficult to say 'no' when asked to perform a task.

A great deal of my own work in helping people reduce their stress in the organizations for which they work involves the teaching of assertiveness.

When faced with a person who is seen to need (or who feels that they need) assertiveness, the helper is usually able to develop an appropriate assertiveness programme. This involves making specific the assertiveness needs of this person, teaching specific assertiveness techniques, practising these techniques and providing the person with feedback about their skills.

Assertiveness training has been shown to be effective for a variety of client groups both in promoting assertiveness and in reducing anxiety. These groups include women (for whom some special programmes have been developed), psychiatric patients, prisoners, homosexuals and nurses.

It should be noted, however, that assertiveness training presupposes that the skill deficiency lies in the person seeking help. Thus a large number of assertiveness programmes have been offered for women based on the assumption that 'if only women were more assertive they could achieve more of that which they wish to achieve, whilst reducing their anxiety'. Yet the social and economic structure of many societies suggests that even if women do become more assertive this may not lead them to be more able to meet their own social, personal and economic needs. That is, the needs which women often express through their attendance at assertiveness training programmes can only be met by social and economic changes, not simply by women modifying their own interpersonal behaviour.

Suggested reading

Ellis, R. and Whittington, D. (1981) *A Guide to Social Skill Training.* London: Croom Helm.
A thorough, if sometimes over-technical and jargonistic introduction to social skills training with some specific examples of training programmes included. Essential to those who wish to study more of the background and rationale for SST.
Meichenbaum, D. (1983) *Coping with Stress.* London: Century Publishing.
An easy-to-read paperback describing the nature of stress and some skill training programmes useful in reducing stress. Includes an anger-reduction programme and some valuable material on the relationship between stress and ill health.
Trower, P., Bryant, B. and Argyle, M. (1978) *Social Skills and Mental Health.* London: Methuen.
A thoroughly detailed introduction and description of a variety of SST programmes together with a detailed review of research. Not an easy read, but worth working through if you intend to make extensive use of SST in your helping activities.

Lange, A. and Jakubowski, P. (1976) *Responsible Assertive Behaviour*. Illinois: Research Press.

Of the many books on assertiveness training available, this seems to me the most useful to the practitioner. It includes a detailed statement of rationale and some examples of training programmes.

Meichenbaum, D. and Jaremko, M. (1984) *Stress Prevention and Management*. New York: Plenum Press.

A thorough introduction to the ideas, procedures and research on stress inoculation and management programmes. Makes extensive use of case examples.

Falloon, I., Lindley, P. and McDonald, R. (1974) *Social Training – A Manual*. London: Maudsley Hospital.

If you intend working with SST on communication related difficulties, this practical guide will be invaluable. It offers detailed programme descriptions and suggestions as well as some illustrations of the way in which such programmes have been used. You may have difficulty obtaining it, but it will be worth the effort.

Liberman, R. (1975) *Personal Effectiveness*. Illinois: Research Press.

Describes some useful activities aimed at the promotion of active coping. In particular, the book does well in its introduction of the idea of contracting.

Chapter 6

Helping and Thinking

What are the skills the helper can use in their attempts to modify or change the way in which a person thinks about themselves when they are experiencing some distress? Using a method of helping developed by Albert Ellis, a major figure in the history of psychotherapy and counselling, I now consider: (a) the way in which irrational thinking and beliefs contribute to the experience of distress; (b) the way in which helpers can understand the irrational nature of many of the beliefs those in distress hold; (c) the methods by which a helper can affect the beliefs and self-talk patterns of a person in need; and (d) some of the uses of this form of helping, illustrated by case study materials. I shall emphasize the idea that self-talk patterns shape a person's emotional response to a situation in a way that determines his or her actions.

As with social skills training, helpers who seek to directly affect the thinking of a person in need often find themselves acting as teachers. Counselling for rationality is often a didactic process which is more directive/informative than facilitative. A great deal of social skills training is concerned with modifying behaviour through coaching and feedback. In contrast, a great deal of rational –emotive work is concerned with modifying thinking through confrontation, coaching and feedback. For this type of counselling and helping to be effective, the helper has to make a careful assessment of the thinking patterns of the person in need and should develop a climate of trust in which the confrontation, coaching and feedback processes can be undertaken in a way that promotes change rather than mistrust.

Two forms of self appraisal

Albert Ellis distinguishes between two ways in which people evaluate themselves. The first he calls *rational beliefs*. When people see or appraise themselves in this way they are not regarding themselves or their social world in absolute terms. Their needs are expressed as desires, preferences or wishes rather than in statements of 'musts', 'shoulds', 'oughts' or 'have tos'. Those who appraise themselves rationally experience pleasure when their desires are met; they experience mild displeasure (sadness, annoyance or concern) when their needs are not met. But this sadness and concern does not over-power or consume them – they develop further preferences and modify their thinking to take account of their recent experiences. Thus, rational appraisers can be seen to:

- have a high acceptance and tolerance of ambiguity
- be self-directing and self-correcting
- be flexible
- be self-interested in a way that accounts for their social roles
- be accepting of feedback which is not always positive.

In contrast, there are those who appraise themselves irrationally and use irrational beliefs to guide their thinking. The core of their thinking 'style' is their perception of reality in absolute terms. Rather than thinking of their needs in terms of preferences or wishes, they think of their needs in terms of 'musts', 'shoulds' and 'oughts'. What begins in their thinking as a desire (for example, the desire to be successful) is soon translated into an imperative (that is, 'I must be successful'). When they make these demands on them-selves or fail to achieve them they experience negative emotions – depression, guilt, anxiety or anger being the most prevalent. Thus, irrational appraisers can be seen to:

- have a low tolerance for ambiguity and a preference for a 'black and white' world
- be self-interested in a way that tends not to take account of social responsibility
- 'awfulise' their experience of the world because their demands are rarely met to their satisfaction
- employ irrational thinking when considering their situation and rarely appreciate or accept feedback
- experience higher levels of distress than rational appraisers.

Whilst it is psychologically preferable for the person to be a rational appraiser, Ellis suggests that there is a biological tendency to think and act irrationally. This innate tendency is reinforced by a great many messages infants and children receive from parents, schools and other social institutions which are expressed in 'should' and 'must' terms. Thus, the person learns to appraise the world in an irrational way.

Windy Dryden, the leading British rational–emotive psychotherapist, gives an example of this process. Imagine being an 11-year-old girl in a family with three brothers. Father and all three brothers are 'macho-men' – they enjoy hard physical contact sports, they enjoy arguing and fighting, they especially like to tease and be critical of women. The girl experiences all significant males in her life at this age to be aggressive and critical; it is not surprising then that she expects to experience *all* men as aggressive and critical. What is more, she is likely to be upset about this 'reality' – that is, she is likely to 'must-urbate' and 'awfulise' about this fact.

Common irrational beliefs

In developing his approach to helping, Albert Ellis has identified 12 irrational beliefs which he finds are held by those who experience distress and seek his help as a therapist. These are not intended to be an exhaustive list of such irrational beliefs, but, rather, to be indicative of the kinds of beliefs which irrational appraisers hold and 'must-urbate' and 'awfulise' about.

• It is a dire necessity that I be loved or approved of by everyone for everything I do.

• Certain acts are wrong and evil and those who perform these acts should be severely punished.

• It is terrible, horrible, and catastrophic when things are not the way I would like them to be.

• Unhappiness is caused by external events – it is forced upon one by external events, other people and circumstances.

• If something is or maybe dangerous or fearsome, I should be terribly concerned about it.

• It is easier to avoid or replace life's difficulties than to face up to them.

• I need someone or something stronger or greater than myself upon which I can rely.

• I should be thoroughly competent, adequate and achieving in all the things I do and should be recognized as such.

• Because something in my past strongly affected my life, it should indefinitely affect it.

• What other people do is vitally important to my existence and I should therefore make great efforts to change them to be more like

the people I would like them to be.
- Human happiness can be achieved by inertia and inaction.
- I have virtually no control over my emotions and I just cannot help feeling certain things.

Ellis suggests that someone who holds one of these beliefs and behaves as if this belief was a guiding feature of their life will experience distress. Let me illustrate this point with a particular case study.

Mike is a thrusting and ambitious middle range executive with a large multi-national computer company. From the time he started school until his first year with the company he has been regarded as a 'high-flyer' – his performance appraisals at university and in the company have been excellent and he always expects to be top of the class or the best amongst his category of workers at any time. He was appointed executive project director for a project that the company regards as risky and difficult. Mike took on the project and was confident – he expects to be thoroughly competent and achieving in all the things he does and does not expect to fail or experience undue difficulty. Indeed, he has told his family that he must succeed in the post he now holds since it is the company's 'big test' of his ability. In fact the company has asked Mike to undertake the task because they think that 'if anyone can do it, Mike can' but 'they don't think it can be done'. In other words the company express confidence in Mike even if the project is not successful.

The project is going badly. None of the production requirements can be met on time and the quality of the product is poor. Mike feels unhappy because external events are forcing him to be a failure. He also feels anxious that a failure on this project might lead to his dismissal from the company. He decides not to tell them of the gradually worsening situation in the hope that 'things will get better'. Mike experiences this situation as 'one of the most stressful things in his life' – he frequently says that he 'feels life just isn't worth living'...'It is truly awful'.

This brief case illustration shows four irrational beliefs at work: (a) the competent and achieving belief; (b) the 'I have no control' belief; (c) the avoid rather than act belief and (d) the 'isn't it awful?' belief. The fact that Mike holds and works with these beliefs is what creates

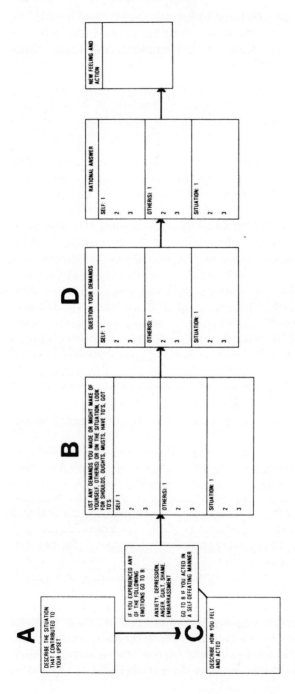

Figure 1. Examining irrational beliefs through the A–B–C–D process. (Adapted from Windy Dryden *Individual Psychotherapy in Britain*. London: Harper and Row. With permission.)

his distress, which takes the form of feeling anxious and awful. The situation is not as 'black and white' as Mike wishes it to be, but he behaves and thinks as if it were. The beliefs he holds about the situation shape his response to it and lead him to create his own distress.

The point to note here is that holding one of the 12 irrational beliefs listed is likely to lead to the experience of some distress or unhappiness, since the accepting of the belief leads the person to 'must-urbate' or 'awfulise' what is happening to them. It is not the event or other people that create the distress, it is the way in which one thinks about the event or others that leads to distressing experiences.

A-B-C-D

Ellis suggests that the 'mechanism' by which thoughts shape emotional responses and action in respect of some situation can be understood in terms of a simple model. In this model there is some activating event (A), such as a challenge from another person or a new situation at home or a sudden self-realization of some kind; there are the consequences (C) for the person of their experience of the event – sadness, pride, pleasure, anger, guilt, excitement, enjoyment or whatever; and there are beliefs (B) about the event which shape the person's reaction to it – such as the irrational beliefs listed above, or more rational versions of those beliefs. Ellis suggests that the consequences (C) of some event (A) are produced by means of the beliefs (B) the person holds about the event.

Figure 1 illustrates this more clearly. In this figure, designed by Windy Dryden as an aid to working with those who seek help because they are experiencing distress, the person is first asked to describe the situation or event which most contributed to their distress. In essence, this is a description of the activating event (A). They are then asked to describe as exactly as they can their response to this event in terms of both feelings and behaviours. This requires them to focus upon the consequences (C) of the event for them. If this last description produces descriptions of anxiety, depression, anger, guilt, shame, embarrassment or a similar emotion or a self-defeating coping response, the person is asked to describe in detail the 'must', 'ought', 'should', 'got to' or 'have to' statements that were a part of their 'self-talk' during their response and to examine the way in which they appraised the situation and others in these same terms. The aim of such an activity is to diagnose the thinking which led them to experience distress and to demonstrate to them the link between the B and the C of their experience.

This simple diagram reveals the essential feature of the rational–emotive approach which helpers need to understand: it is not events which create distress, it is the reactions of individuals to these events which 'produce' distress. This reaction depends crucially upon the kinds of appraisal the person has of that event and of themselves. In the end, it is this appraisal which will shape their response.

The task of the helper who seeks to change the beliefs and appraisals of the person in need is to modify the thinking and belief system of the person. This is done by disputing the beliefs – disputing being the D referred to in the title of this section.

The prerequisites of effective helping to change thinking

To be able to dispute the beliefs and thoughts a person has requires some skill and considerable practice. It also requires the helpers to have a clear and specific contract. I now emphasize the three prerequisites for working effectively to change the way people appraise themselves and their social situation.

First, the helper needs to build a *relationship* with the person in need which is accepting and trusting. There is no one way of establishing such bonds – some of those seeking help prefer their helper to be cool and distant so that they can trust them, others prefer genuineness and empathy to be shown symbolically through humour. The helper needs to maintain a flexible approach to the development of affective bonds. One point here: Albert Ellis does not regard warmth as a key feature of helping relationships directed towards changing the person's thinking. He suggests that excessive warmth reinforces the dependency needs of those seeking help and makes the confronting and teaching tasks of rational–emotive work more rather than less difficult.

Second, there is a need for the helper and the person in need to agree upon the *goals* of their work. As with SST and crisis work, there is a need for a contract. The helper needs to encourage the person in need to distinguish between realistic and unrealistic goals, and between goals which are self-defeating and goals which are self-enhancing. Setting out a contract and making goals explicit is one way of encouraging the person to take responsibility for their own development. It is also a way of demystifying the counselling and helping process.

Windy Dryden suggests that, in addition to the need for a contract about goals, there is a need for contracts about tasks. He suggests that helpers have the following tasks:

- to help those in need recognize that their own thinking is a major source of their distress
- to help those in need identify and change their irrational thoughts through teaching and coaching
- to teach those in need that the methods used in rational–emotive work are effective in achieving and maintaining changes in thinking.

He also suggests that those seeking help need to agree on the following tasks:

- to observe their own emotional and behavioural disturbance
- to examine for themselves the relationship between their thinking, feelings and behaviour
- to continually work, under the direction of their helper, on changing their irrational and distorted thinking so as to promote their own psychological health and well-being.

Dryden suggests that agreement on these tasks involves the person in need making a direct commitment to work in a particular way and that this is in itself a valuable step on the route to more rational thinking. It also provides a vehicle for the helper to examine the behaviour of the person in need; if they make a contract and then break it the helper can infer that they are not only thinking irrationally but behaving delinquently.

Promoting rational thinking

A variety of techniques have been developed which helpers can use when seeking to change the thinking of a person in need. In this chapter I summarize these methods briefly. All of them involve the helper: (a) showing the link between thinking and distress; (b) seeking to emphasize the need to think more rationally; (c) being persistent in pursuing the irrational thought(s) that lead someone to seek help – one writer describes this as the helper 'fighting and pounding away at the faulty belief system, time and again'; and (d) providing accurate feedback to the person as to the extent of change they have achieved.

Some of the techniques that the helper may find useful include:

Disputing irrational beliefs. The helper demonstrates that the distress a person is experiencing is a direct result of the beliefs that they hold. The beliefs are challenged by the helper asking questions such as:

- where is the evidence that supports your beliefs?
- why do you experience such distress from the way you think?
- why is the situation so terrible or awful – why isn't it merely tough or unfortunate?
- why do you make the assumption that your experience of this situation in some way marks you down for the rest of your life?

Essentially, disputing is a way of highlighting through critical questioning the fact that the beliefs the person holds about some reality have little relationship to reality. The helper needs to be challenging and direct and should ensure that the person in need accepts that their motives are genuine.

Homework. The helper sets the person in need some homework tasks. These can vary, depending upon the need the person has. Some examples of tasks include:

- asking the person to read some books that emphasize the ideas of rational–emotive work – a list of these is provided at the end of this chapter
- learning written statements and repeating them a number of times each day, especially in situations in which they often find themselves thinking and acting irrationally
- working with others to identify their irrational beliefs and their consequences
- completing diaries documenting each occasion on which they use self-talk involving 'shoulds', 'musts', 'oughts' or 'got tos'
- the person in need disputing their own irrational belief in writing for 10 minutes each day – the aim being to encourage them to 'give up' their own irrational belief and replace it with a more rational belief through their own efforts.

Such homework assignments are regarded as especially important in (a) demonstrating commitment to the process of self-help under the guidance of a helper; (b) creating a strong a personal basis for changing irrational thoughts; and (c) sustaining work the helper undertakes during contact sessions.

Emotive–evocative techniques. The range of techniques here is varied. All of them are vivid ways of providing the helper with the resources to dispute irrational beliefs. Appropriate techniques include:

- shame attacking – the person in need is encouraged to undertake some task which they find difficult but not hurtful (for example, to return a bottle of wine at a restaurant, or to collect up goods in a supermarket which they cannot pay for, or to wear odd shoes for a day) and are then asked to examine just what was involved in their experience of this activity – the idea being that they can be encouraged to recognize that, whilst this situation was difficult for them, it was not awful or terrible

• rational–emotive imagery – the person is encouraged, under conditions of relaxation (see Chapter 8), to imagine themselves in the situation they find difficult and to explore the implication of being in that situation whilst holding a rational belief about it. The most important technique used in this category concerns the helpers themselves. Helpers working in this way show the client that it is alright to be natural and 'themselves' during helping sessions; helpers avoid seeking approval from those they are seeking to help; they do not live by or make use of 'shoulds', 'musts', 'oughts' or 'got tos'. Finally, they are willing to risk themselves by continuing to challenge the irrational beliefs of those they are helping. In these ways the helper acts as a role model to the person in need.

Techniques aimed at thinking and behaviour. Methods derived from behavioural techniques (see Chapter 5) have been extensively adapted and used in this form of helping. In particular, the following techniques have been widely used:

• 'stay in there' activities, in which the person in need is asked to perform an activity they dislike – like swearing or crawling on the floor – for as long as possible during a helping session so that the helper and the person can explore how discomfort arises from their patterns of thinking
• skills training – extending the use of some of the SST techniques described in the previous chapter to thinking
• role-playing and role rehearsal.

Applications

These techniques and the general approach have been used in a great many different situations:

• reducing the exam anxiety of anxious pupils and students
• reducing the fear of flying
• reducing public speaking anxiety
• preparing patients for surgery
• enabling candidates to approach job interviews in a less stressful way

- reducing conflicts between marital partners
- changing the quality of staff relations in an organization ... and many more.

There is some limited evidence that individualized helping is more successful than group helping using these methods. But rational–emotive work has been used in groups for assertiveness training, marriage preparation, parent effectiveness education and stress reduction. Indeed, there is now an extensive literature documenting its applicability to a variety of settings (schools, hospitals, police work, social work, marriage guidance) and client groups, to suggest that the approach is a substantial and growing way of working with those in need.

Suggested reading

Dryden, W. (1984) *Rational Emotive Therapy: Fundamentals and Innovations.* London: Croom Helm.
In this short (and expensive) book, the author describes in more detail than has been possible here the basic ideas of RET and offers descriptions of more advanced RET techniques. In addition he introduces some developments of RET which he claims are innovative and shows how these work in practice by reference to case examples. The book is not easy to read (largely because of the way the book was printed), but is worth working through.

Ellis, A. (1962) *Reason and Emotion in Psychotherapy.* New Jersey: Lyle Stuart.
Do not be put off by the inclusion of 'psychotherapy' in the title of this book. It is an easy to read, lucid account of the basic philosophy of RET and its applications. It is written by the founder of RET and, in his typical style, is witty and imaginative as well as practical.

Walen, S., DiGiuseppe, R. and Wessler, P. (1980) *Practitioners' Guide to Rational Emotive Therapy.* New York: Oxford University Press.
Of the books listed here, this is by far the best and most useful practical guide for the beginning practitioner of RET. Step by step the authors introduce principles and procedures in a way that makes RET attractive, humane, and a workable method for counselling and helping.

Ellis, A. and Becker, I. (1982) *A Guide to Personal Happiness.* California: Wiltshire.
This book is intended for the person in need. It is used by helpers as a homework assignment (see text) and as such is very valuable.

Chapter 7

Helping and Feelings

A great many people think of counselling and helping as being primarily concerned with emotions and feelings. This is because they associate helping with distress, anxiety, depression or some other difficulty which shows itself through the emotions a person in need displays and experiences. As we have seen, however, counselling and helping can also be concerned with thinking and social behaviour. In the end, all forms of helping are concerned with thinking, behaviour *and* feelings since these three features of the person are inextricably linked. For helping and counselling are about the whole person and their well-being. My definition of helping and counselling (see Chapter 1) emphasizes the role of the helper in enabling the person to live the life they wish to lead without being more dependant than they wish to be upon others. In essence, helping and counselling are concerned with the promotion of actions which benefit and give comfort to the person in need without abusing the rights of others. The term 'action' implies thinking, behaviour and feelings.

There are times when the focus of helping is more upon feelings than upon thinking or behaviour. On these occasions the counsellor or helper feels that it is necessary to examine feelings directly. This arises when:

- a person is unable to discriminate between the different feelings they are experiencing
- the person feels unable to think straight because their feelings are getting in the way
- the person is experiencing new feelings and powerful emotions which they seek help in understanding
- when the person feels that their feelings are no longer under their own control.

On these occasions, which may occur during the course of an ongoing helping relationship or may be the beginning point of such a relationship, the helper will wish the person in need to better understand and be able to 'manage' feelings.

A number of practical ways of helping a person look at their emotions and feelings are now introduced. Some of the ideas behind these procedures are also examined so that you are able to make connections between the practice of helping and its psychological roots. The substance of this chapter is based on what is known as *Gestalt* (pronounced ghest-alt) counselling.

For the methods outlined here to be effective, the helper needs to develop and sustain a helping relationship which is founded upon the conditions outlined in detail on pp 15-35. A helping strategy based upon the releasing of feelings and working with them so as to help the person in need better understand and come to terms with them is essentially a *cathartic* form of helping. The methods outlined here cannot be regarded as a set of mechanical routines which the helper can apply without reference to the significant (and sometimes immediate) impact they have upon the person they are helping.

Starting points

When feelings are the focus of a helping relationship, then what is usually happening is that the person in need is not fully aware of the link between their feelings and their thoughts and behaviours. That is, they are not fully 'in tune with' or aware of their own feelings and their impact.

This observation provides a starting point for the use of feeling-focused helping activity. The aim of the helper is to encourage the person in need to attend to their feelings whilst at the same time connecting these feelings to their understanding of themselves as a person in the social world. Feelings are not examined or explored in the abstract by the helper; on the contrary, the whole purpose of exploring a person's feelings is to enable them to have more awareness of what it *means* to have those feelings and what others feel when they interact with them.

Feelings become a central concern of the helper when the person in need is no longer sure which feelings are predominant at any one time or when the person acts irrespective of the feelings they are experiencing. Most frequently, feelings become the issue when the person in need seeks to comply with what they regard as social

demands by disregarding their own feelings: the person is so concerned to be well liked in the circles in which they move (or in their
marriage or at work) that they disregard even strong emotions in
order to be seen to be acceptable or successful. Here is an example
of some of my own work with Sam, who has precisely this problem.

Sam: ... I suppose what gets me anxious is having to, well I don't
know, er, perform all the time ... like I sometimes feel that I'm
expected to be someone who is lively and funny and enthusiastic
all the time, like, er, even when I'm feeling pissed off others want
me to be 'lively Sam, the life and soul of the party'. So I start to
perform and everyone else feels that I must be a really nice guy,
but inside I feel like a shell, a kind of oyster that's been picked at
by some gourmet crowd and laughed at ... it makes me feel angry,
but I also feel trapped ...

Me: You feel as if you're trapped in an empty shell and being made
to perform like an oyster ...

Sam: Yeah, that's it ... I don't know who I am any more, I just seem
to have to be what others want me to be ...

Me: OK, let's try something Sam. You say that you feel trapped
inside a shell with everyone making you perform ...

Sam: Right.

Me: OK, I want you to sit on the floor and be that oyster in the shell.
(Sam hesitantly sits on the floor.) OK, now all I want you to do
is to tell me ... to repeat back to me the messages you get from
other people, OK? Right, do it Sam – send me the messages you
get from other people...

Sam: OK, my mom says 'You gotta be a success, boy, after all the
hard work you put into school and we put into you ...'

Me: OK, mom says 'we want you to succeed because we worked
hard so that you could ...'

Sam: Sally *(girlfriend)* says 'Come on Sam, be fun ... that's why I
like you'.

Me: OK, Sally says if you're not fun I won't like you.

Sam: Mike *(best friend)* says 'I call you whenever I feel low so that
I can feel good again – so be entertaining, be spontaneous'.

Me: So Mike gives you the classic imperative – I want you to be
spontaneous, so do it now or else!

Sam: (suddenly stands up) You've turned each one of these statements into a 'no-win for Sam' statement haven't you? *(talking
directly at me)*

Me: Yes, on the basis of the inflections of your voice.

Sam: Shit! That's it. If I don't do as they expect, I think I am going to lose my friends and all that, and if I do what they expect then I feel as if I am losing me, is that what you're trying to tell me, Steve?

Me: How can you be lost when you're nothing but an empty shell, Sam?

Sam: Hey, I'm not an empty shell ...

Me: You were a minute ago, what has happened now to let me see Sam?

This brief extract from a long session illustrates the way in which the helper seeks to elicit strong feelings during the course of a helping session so that the feelings the person in need is struggling with can be 'at the surface'.

When the person acts in disregard of their feelings they can be said to be *unintegrated*: they have not integrated an important and significant part of themselves. They can also be said to be functioning at a social level only – their emotional world is being denied and constrained in a way that is likely to give rise to tensions, anxiety and (in certain circumstances) physical pain. Once the person begins to ignore feelings in this way they find it difficult to take full account of them. Here is an example.

Sally's father died when she was 16. Her mother never fully explained what had happened to her father and Sally repressed her feelings of loss and worked hard to please her mother. Later, Sally became acutely aware of the implications (personal and emotional) of not having a father but had spent so many years repressing her feelings that she is now frightened and concerned by her anxiety about examining these feelings. These emotions are so strong that she is depressed. What depresses her is the feeling that it is essential that she examine what it means for her to have lost her father but that she cannot do so without experiencing more pain than she can bear. In her words 'I am trapped by my own emotions'.

To help Sally and others like her come to terms with their feelings and enhance their own awareness, the helper needs to avoid certain behaviours. In particular, the helper needs to avoid lengthy discussions about past feelings or feelings which occurred long before the person began to seek help. Such talk unduly encourages the person to see feelings as historical experiences rather than emotions experienced in the present. For a similar reason the helper needs to discourage talk about what *could* have been, *should* have been, *might* have been in the past, or similar speculation about the future. Such talk avoids dealing with emotions and feelings in the 'here and now' of the interaction between the helper and the person in need and is a way of making feelings intellectual rather than emotional experiences. Finally, the helper needs to avoid manipulating the person in need to experience and react to feelings which they do not in fact possess. No matter how empathic the helper might feel, they cannot know what the person is feeling – they can only approximate the feeling experiences of those they seek to help.

To help the person to examine and reintegrate their feelings there are certain positive behaviours the helper can engage in. These include:

- paying concrete attention to detail – the helper needs to ensure that no feature of their interaction goes unnoticed by them, since all of their interactions constitute an emotional experience
- encouraging the person to engage in activities which enable them to directly examine their emotions – don't just talk about feelings, explore them actively using some of the methods and processes outlined below
- encourage the person in need to accept responsibility for their own behaviour – enable them to stop denying their feelings, pretending to experience something, displacing their emotions or blaming others.

Facing up to emotions

These basic features of feeling-focused work can be elaborated in a series of statements about the method by which helpers can help the person in need face up to and reintegrate their emotions. The first of those statements is that the helper should always focus upon the *here and now* – upon what is happening in the helping relationship rather than upon what is happening outside that relationship. The basic reason for suggesting this is that talk about past emotions is distorted through selective perception and selective remembering: the person recalls that which is least painful and that which is felt to be 'appropriate' for the helper to hear. A similar difficulty arises with statements about emotions the person hopes to experience in the future. Most commonly, individuals seeking help project themselves as having catastrophic emotional experiences or exceptionally pleasant ones: rarely are the fantasies an individual has about future emotions realized exactly. Since the aim of the helper is to promote awareness, this aim of helping can best be achieved by focusing upon the extent to which the person is aware in the present, that is, during the course of a session with a helper.

No 'whys'

The second method statement concerns the way the helper deals with the 'why' questions which those in need often ask – 'Why am I the way I am?', 'Why do I get so angry with myself?', or 'Why will this pain inside me never stop?'. Almost all 'why' questions of this type lead the helper to answer with 'because ...', and the process of dealing with emotions and feelings thus becomes intellectualized. Indeed, most 'why–because' conversations lead the person in need to argue 'yes–but', thus further intellectualizing the conversation. So as to avoid this sequence of talk, the helper is encouraged to focus upon the *what* and *how* of behaviour. If the person is encouraged to be aware of what they are doing and how they do it, then they are in a good position to make decisions about whether they are going to continue to do it. This quotation from Arnold Beisser makes this point very clear:

> ... change occurs when one becomes what he is, not when he tries to become what he is not. Change does not take place through a coercive attempt by the individual or another person to change him, but it does take place if one takes the time and effort to be what he is.

Thus by drawing attention to the *what* and *how* of a person's behaviour, the helper is encouraging the person to be more of what they already are – to be more aware of themselves.

Activities

A third method statement concerns the activities which the helper may wish to engage in. A great deal of helping involves talk – just talk. In seeking to understand feelings as they are experienced the helper may want the person to engage in some specific activities which bring up or show up emotions. Some of these activities are described below. The helper needs to be careful about the way in which these activities are used. They are not party games. They are helping devices that enable the helper to focus upon what the person in need is experiencing when he or she experiences it. The 'trick' of these activities is not to talk about them in some abstract way, but to describe what was experienced as exactly as possible. Through such description the person is enabled to become aware of their feelings and their relevance.

Owning emotions

Often, the person in need externalizes their feelings – they treat their feelings as if they were not part of but apart from their self. For example, Jackie says that her headaches often prevent her from 'having a good time' and she feels frustrated that her headaches 'do this' to her. Jackie thinks of her 'symptom' (the headaches) as if it were external to her and as something over which she has no control. A fourth method statement concerns just such a feature of the person's behaviour. It is that the helper should encourage the person in need to own and identify with their feelings, their symptoms and their behaviour. For example, Jackie is asked to own her own headache by saying 'I am Jackie's headache and as such I prevent Jackie from feeling that it is possible to have a good time'. Essentially, this statement concerns language and semantics: the helper is asking the person in need to stop saying 'it' and to start saying 'I'. Here are some examples of this in action: instead of saying 'my hand – it is trembling' we encourage the person to say 'I am trembling'; instead of saying 'my voice sounds like it is crying' we encourage the person to say 'I am crying'. By doing so the aim is to encourage the person in need to accept responsibility for their feelings and their bodies and to enable them to integrate their feelings and the way in which they think about themselves.

This last method statement can be illustrated by an extract from a counselling session. Here is an extract of Lois talking with Jim – Jim is the counsellor.

Jim: What are you aware of now, right now?
Lois: I am aware that I am talking to you and that I am nervous, shy. I can feel that I am tense at the back of my neck and I get anxious about this.
Jim: Describe this anxiety – how do you experience it?
Lois: My voice – it quivers a bit ...
Jim: Can you say, 'I am my voice and I am quivering ...'
Lois: ... now I can feel my eyes looking away.
Jim: Lois, take responsibility for your eyes.
Lois: I am my eyes. I find it difficult to look at you and I am my voice and I am still quivering and I am my hand which is shaking a little.

In this extract, the beginning part of a helping session in which Lois was seeking to come to terms with her feelings of failure in marriage, the helper encourages the person in need to describe their feelings in the first person rather than the third. They are seeking to ensure that the person owns their feelings and that they are fully aware of their meaning and place in their behaviour.

This extract from a counselling session leads us to the fifth and final method statement to be mentioned here. It is that the helper should encourage the person in need at every opportunity to accept full responsibility for their actions. Instead of denying their own responsibility, suggesting that they were made to act in a particular way because of other people, or projecting their feelings onto other people ('It is not me that's angry, it's her ...') the person is encouraged to accept their thoughts, feelings and actions as part of themselves. Often those seeking help from a counsellor or helper are looking for a way of changing the consequences of their behaviour without changing the behaviour itself. They blame others or some historical feature of themselves, such as some childhood experience or a poor decision about marriage partners. As long as they attribute responsibility for their behaviour to another person or to some concept (for example, 'It's just the stress of the job') then they remain powerless to change their situation – they give their power to this other person or the concept. The helper needs to ensure that the person understands this principle and that they learn to do their own work, take their own risks and accept responsibility for their own lives and actions. By so doing, the helper will encourage the person to discover what he or she is capable of.

These five method statements are intended to illuminate the ideas behind some of the techniques to be described below. Two words of caution. First, as was emphasized at the beginning of this chapter, the helper engaging in work concerned directly with feelings is likely to encounter a great deal of material which the person will find difficult and distressing to share. It is therefore essential that the helper understands that the techniques to be described here are described in the context of a sustained helping relationship. Secondly, the value of these techniques is that they provide the helper with some broad ideas about how to put the principles just elaborated into practice. They are not a set of routines which will produce awareness or dramatic change just because they have been carried out exactly as described here. The basis on which these techniques are most often used is to extend, elaborate, or highlight what is already happening between the helper and the person in need.

They are *not* themselves an adequate basis for a helping relationship.

The techniques described here are varied. Some derive from drama work and others from *Gestalt* counselling. All have been developed by helpers working in a variety of settings. You will need to decide for yourself which of these ways of working is most suited to you as a person and the style of helping you engage in. The choice of tactic needs to be conscious: these methods work best when the helper fully understands the basis of the helping strategy they are using and has confidence in the value of the specific tactic they are employing in pursuit of this strategy.

Language use

One set of activities which the helper can usefully use in their attempts to encourage the person to recognize and accept their own feelings involves the use of language. Already mentioned is the need to discourage the person in need from referring to their bodies or their feelings as 'it' and to encourage them to use 'I' statements when expressing their feelings or referring to their bodies.

An extension of this principle is to require the person to speak as much as possible in the first person singular. Statements which begin with the phrases 'I want ...' or 'I feel ...' or 'I see ...' express both what is happening to the person and suggest the fact that the person is willing to own these experiences. This sounds relatively straightforward, but many of those seeking help find this difficult. For example, Jack is finding his work very stressful. He makes the following statements during the course of the first seven minutes of an interview with a helper at work:

'We all know that my kind of work is demanding and stressful ...'
'You can't expect a company of the size of this to understand my needs and to respond to them in a sympathetic manner – they have their profits to think of ...'
'Well, it's the typical behaviour of middle executives towards us up and rising junior executives, isn't it?'

Jack owns none of these statements. He is encouraged by his helper to examine each of them carefully and to rephrase them in the first person. He says:

'I have always thought that the work I do is stressful to me ...'
'I do not expect large companies to care for individuals'

'I find middle executives dislike and feel antagonistic towards me ...'

Through this rephrasing, Jack is encouraged to regard his feelings and reactions as his and therefore to regard them as something he can do something about.

A second language 'device' that is helpful for this same reason requires the person seeking help to stop 'broadcasting' – that is, to stop speaking as if they were an announcer on a local radio station being listened to only by the helper. Instead of saying 'It's really quiet here today', I encourage those with whom I work to say, 'Stephen, you're not saying much to me', so as to make clear that I am not an audience – I am a particular person behaving in a particular way. This same request will be made whenever the person treats me like an audience for a radio station.

A third, and very important language device that is appropriate to this form of helping is to suggest to the person in need that they should stop saying 'can't' and substitute 'won't'. For example, Roberta often begins to react to suggestions that I might make by saying 'But I can't say that to my mother ...' (even though Roberta is 36 and has a lot she wants to say to her mother). She is pushed to accept responsibility for her decision not to say something to her mother by saying 'I won't say that to my mother'. This simple change of words makes a significant difference to the way in which she and others view themselves as taking responsibility for their own actions and the feelings which accompany them. This is a small device, but it stops the person accrediting their actions to a state of helplessness.

Finally here, I discourage the person in need from asking questions. Questions, such as 'Why do I feel ...?' often confuse communications rather than clarify them and lead to games such as those mentioned briefly above. In addition to focusing upon the *what* and *how* of behaviour, the helper needs to encourage the person to make statements rather than ask questions. Whenever a question occurs to them ask them to make it into a statement. For example, instead of saying 'Why am I still so angry at you?' encourage the person to answer their own (unsaid) question with a statement like 'I am still angry at you because I have asked you twice to do something and you have yet to do it'. This adds to responsibility taking and further enhances awareness.

An empty chair

One device used frequently in the attempt to encourage the person to recognize and accept feelings and to take responsibility for them follows from the observation that many of those who present themselves to a helper are carrying two self-talk messages within them. The nature of these two messages will vary from person to person, but frequently occurring messages include:

- 'It's wrong even to think about x but I can see myself doing x – what should I do?'
- 'I should feel this ... but I feel something else – isn't this awful?'
- 'Everyone expects me to ... but I feel like I want to ...'

These self-talk statements can give rise to anxiety and self-doubt (see Chapter 6); they are also frequently indicative of the extent to which the person has intellectualized their own feelings. The helper's task is to encourage them to re-enact their self-talk but to be honest and direct about this dialogue. In short, the person in need is asked to hold a conversation between these two 'parts' of themselves. It is helpful to ask the person to hold this dialogue between him or herself and an empty chair – the empty chair symbolizing that side of the self-talk they feel most removed from at the beginning of the dialogue process. As the dialogue proceeds, the person is encouraged to physically move position between the two chairs whenever he or she feels that the 'other chair' best represents the strength of the argument they are putting at any particular moment.

As an example of this, Dorothy chose to use the empty chair as a way of coming to terms with the fact that she had not said things to her mother just before her mother's death which she had wanted to say and felt awkward about doing so. I encouraged Dorothy to regard one chair as her saying 'I must tell mother these things ...' and the other chair as Dorothy saying 'I will not tell mother these things ...'. Dorothy begain her dialogue with her self in this last chair but, as the dialogue became more heated, Dorothy switched between the two chairs with some frequency. The scene became very emotional. Dorothy was struggling with her fear of her mother on the one hand and her fear of leaving unfinished business in the air if her mother died before she (Dorothy) was able to say things to her that she felt were important concerning her feelings of guilt about her mother's illness (which she felt indirectly responsible for). As a result of failing to resolve this argument between the two 'parts' of her 'self' at the appropriate time, Dorothy has spent a lot of time since her mother's death feeling guilty both about her mother and about her own failure to meet her own emotional needs.

The procedure outlined here helped clarify and ease both of these feelings of guilt. The role of the helper throughout this activity was directed at encouraging Dorothy to reflect all of the thoughts and feelings inside her and to enable Dorothy to 'lose herself' in the dialogue – to experience it fully.

This same technique can be used by the person in need to have a conversation with a person who is associated with their difficulty but is not present at the time of the helping session. For example, a colleague used the empty chair technique in marriage guidance counselling:

> A woman sought his help in understanding her reactions to the sexual demands of her husband. She felt that she could not talk directly to her husband about the feelings his sexual demands gave rise to, but did agree to talk to the empty chair as if it were him. After some time (about 15 minutes), she began to occupy her husband's 'empty chair' and to talk back to herself. The conversation soon switched from sexuality to matters concerning the degree of intimacy between them across a variety of features of their marriage.

This person claims that this one experience of helping – which lasted about two hours in all – enabled her to see clearly what was happening to her and how was letting it happen. It also illuminated for her the way in which her own behaviour towards her husband supported her husband's behaviour towards her.

A further variation of the empty chair technique occurs when the helper, fully understanding the parts being played by the person in need, occupies one of the chairs and continues the dialogue as if they were the other part of the conversation. For this to be effective, the helper requires a high degree of empathy with the person in need. The person being helped also needs to be prepared for such an eventuality at the time such a tactic is beginning to be employed.

In my own experience, one of the most effective uses of this device I have seen concerned a 15-year-old girl who was trying to make a critical choice about her career. She was not sure what route to take; her mother was pushing her to think of a career in science; her father was encouraging her not to think of a career at all, but instead was wanting her to settle down and get married; one school teacher was strongly arguing that she should follow a career in languages; whilst the careers teacher was encouraging her to look at career opportunities in computing. The helper working with this girl used a chair for each of these 'arguments' and pushed the girl hard to develop an argument with each of the chairs in the room. The result was that the girl chose to do something that was not on the agenda at the beginning of this process, namely to study for a business qualification in marketing. The process in this case involved the girl arguing with each chair in turn, and sometimes countering the argument from one chair with the views of another. She said she could do this 'because it was safe' to explore these different feelings and because she couldn't upset anyone. Why it was effective as a helping tactic on this occasion was that it brought out for this girl her need to make up her own mind in a way that was respectful of the motives of these other persons, if not of their advice. It seemed to enhance her own awareness of her self whilst at the same time strengthening her feeling that she had to accept responsibility for her self and the decisions that she made.

Exaggeration

When the person in need thinks they recognize a feeling, such as anger or guilt or excitement, but is not sure how this feeling is influencing their thoughts and actions, the helper can encourage understanding by asking the person to exaggerate the emotion. For example, when someone says that they are angry with their husband because he spends so much time with his friends and so little time at home, the helper might encourage this person to really exaggerate her feelings – shouting and being abusive, throwing cushions at her husband (or an empty chair representing her husband if he is not present during the helping session), formulating the most excessive statement of her feeling that she can. The aim of this is to enable the person to recognize the difference between their own feelings and the extreme of that feeling and to develop the skill of being accurate in their assessment of their own feeling level. Exaggeration serves another purpose too. By acting out and dramatizing their feelings the person can see and hear their own feelings as if it were a video of their inner self and can more directly own these feelings.

A further example of exaggeration being used as a tactic in this helping strategy concerns gestures and expressions. In order to direct the person's attention to the link between their feelings and their statements and actions, the helper can draw attention to a movement (such as the wringing of the hands), a posture (such as a slouch in the chair or a tense body posture) or to a phrase the person uses (such as 'I've *got* to ...') and ask them to exaggerate these features of their behaviour and then describe what these features felt like.

A final example of this exaggeration tactic concerns expressions that the person uses. When a person makes a feeling statement which appears significant to the helper but is glossed over by the person in need, the helper can ask them to repeat the statement several times – giving more and more emphasis to it each time it is repeated. This activity – sometimes called graduated exaggeration – enables the person to recognize the extent to which the phrase has meaning for them, whilst at the same time letting them explore the extent to which they feel comfortable with different levels of the phrase's meaning.

All of these exaggeration tactics have a similar purpose: to enable the person in need to recognize the level of their own feelings and the interaction between these feelings and their thoughts and actions.

Reversals

One problem which those in need present when feelings are at the core of their concerns is the inability to express or experience feelings. They say 'I ought to feel happy about this, but I just don't know how to', or 'I ought to be angry about what this is doing to me, but I just can't'. The helper needs to encourage the person to experiment with feelings and their expression in the relatively safe environment of the helping relationship. They can do this by asking the person to act out the emotions they think they should feel (for example, happy or angry as in the examples given here) and to do so as convincingly as they can. The helper then discusses with the person the impact this activity of acting-out has had upon them and asks them to identify the blocks within them to behaving in the way they think and feel to be appropriate. This version of this tactic is often used as an adjunct to the exaggeration tactic just described.

Another form this tactic can take is to ask a person to play the opposite of the role which they usually play. For example, I worked with a person in need who was always subservient and obsequious; I asked them to act aggressively and belligerently towards me whenever they felt that I was not responding to what they were saying or was responding inappropriately. After a few sessions with this instruction being in force the person was able to own and recognize this other feature of themselves and began to be able to use their assertiveness constructively in our relationship. It also became possible for this person to behave more assertively with people in authority – the precise problem which she had presented in the first place.

Rehearsal

Some anxiety about a forthcoming event – a job interview or a specific confrontation or conversation – can be dealt with through a rehearsal of the event itself. The idea is for the helper to give the person in need an opportunity to experience the situation before it happens. Unlike the use of rehearsal in social skills training, the idea here is to encourage the person to experience what it feels like to be in the situation. The intention is not to develop and refine some specific behaviours. Indeed, in the context of working primarily with feelings, the idea is to minimize the use of behaviour routines and to encourage spontaneity.

Such a use of rehearsal raises an interesting point of relevance to all counselling and helping tactics. Though they are presented here as vehicles for achieving specific purposes, the tactics described can be used for a *variety* of purposes with a variety of people at different stages in the development of a helping relationship. The task for the helper is to experiment with these tactics so as to identify the ones with which they are most comfortable and then to develop as many varieties of uses of these tactics as possible. Only then will they be able to match their skills (as demonstrated through the effective use of tactics and strategies) with the needs of the people with whom they are working.

Using dreams

The final tactic concerns dreams. Before describing some of the ways in which dreamwork can be developed for understanding one's feelings you should be aware that this section does not seek to explain how you can interpret dreams. That is another approach to dreamwork altogether. Rather than analyse and interpret the unconscious meaning of a dream (as is the case in psychoanalysis), my concern is to illustrate the ways in which the helper can enable the person with whom they are working to relive their dream – bring it back to life – in such a way as to illuminate some complex features of the person's feelings.

The idea behind this approach is that dreams represent an examination of the person's feelings and thoughts. By reliving the dream and acting it out in consciousness, the person is able to 'get in touch with' or examine their feelings more directly. This is possible because every aspect of the dream is an aspect of the person. The working assumption of the helper should be that all the features of the other people we might dream about or of the situations in which we find ourselves are in fact projections of our own feelings.

Gill is a 23-year-old single girl who has had several relationships with men, each of which has ended in failure and substantial emotional distress. She reports a dream in which one of her ex-boyfriends offers to sell her body for sexual purposes to the man who can suggest the most interesting sexual task for her. The three or four men in the dream then try to outbid each other in terms of the sexual exploits they wish Gill to perform and the bidding is finally won by a man who wants Gill to have anal intercourse with him whilst having oral sex with another. Gill suggests that this dream is disturbing because she finds both the idea and the thought of practising both anal and oral sex unattractive. I asked Gill to act out the process by which her body was sold and Gill created a vivid scene of bids and counter-bids in which she imagined herself having to fulfil such a wide range of sexual acts that she clearly recognized a very sexual part of her self was being 'brought to her' through this dream. She then examined the extent to which sexual demands had played a part in the collapse of her relationships with men. She realized through this process that what had happened in the past was not that she was sexually unresponsive to the men she had had stable relationships with, but that these men were sexually unimaginative and unstimulating for her. She was also able to recognize through her enactment of this dream that her own response to this difficulty had not opened out her own sexuality but had further inhibited the men and had involved her in denying her own sexual needs to her self. Gill then recognized the point in the dream beyond which she felt disgusted – it was the point of sale – and examined the meaning this had for her in terms of the emotions it gave rise to and how these emotions linked to her experiences. It became clear that she had over polarized the choice between limited sex and extreme sex and found herself trapped by feeling unable to make clear her own sexual needs. These things became clear for Gill through her re-enacting this dream.

Another example might be useful here.

Angie is 36, married and the mother of a small child. In her dream she saw her family and her mother walking in a flat and open country in which there was just one tree. In the distance she saw a hurricane approaching very fast. She tried to per-

suade her family and her mother to run to the tree and to hold
on to it as tightly as possible for protection from the hurricane.
At first she had difficulty in communicating with her family
and her mother. Then everyone saw the hurricane and started
to run for the tree. Mother fell and stumbled and the young
child found it difficult to get hold of the tree. Angie tied the
child to the tree with her underskirt and went back for her
mother. By the time Angie had secured her mother to the tree,
the wind was so strong that Angie was blown away and was
never seen again. Angie offered an interpretation of this dream
– she was so busy rescuing other people from the difficulties
of life that she had little time for herself – but she also had an
insight into her own feelings about herself. She knew that her
interpretation felt 'correct', but she learned that she wanted to
be rescued from the situation in which she found herself before
she could stop rescuing others. This insight came from re-
enactment. She discovered through the re-enactment that her
waiting to be rescued was pointless – she had to attend to her
own needs now if she was going to be 'saved' from the weari-
ness she felt from rescuing and looking after others.

Working through dreams by requiring the person to act them out
in detail, playing all the parts and putting this together in a way that
accurately reflects the dream itself is a demanding task for both the
person in need and the helper. However, the results often provide
a powerful basis for helping activity and are a real revealer of inner
emotions. In both of the illustrative examples given here, the use of
the re-enacted dream made substantial differences to both of these
people and made the task of helping that much more rewarding.
However, the helper will often encounter resistance from the person
in need. This takes two forms. First the person will suggest that acting out the dream is difficult or too time-consuming or unrewarding.
The helper, if they feel confident that the dream material may
unlock some feelings which are important to the helping process,
should insist that the dreamwork is undertaken. The second kind of
resistance is to ask for an interpretation from the helper. This should
be avoided. Interpretations and insights gained by the person seeking help are what the helper is looking for – there is no magical lexi-
con of understanding that the helper can offer which is personally
relevant and meaningful to the person in need.

Suggested reading

Stevens, J. (1971) *Awareness – Exploring, Experimenting, Experiencing.* Moab, Utah: Real People Press.
In a lively and provocative text the author examines ways in which some of the ideas briefly introduced in this chapter can be extended and developed. Some more ideas and tactics are introduced.

Chapter 8

Helping and the Body

The body is an important and frequently neglected focus for helping and counselling. The body often provides the first indications of stress – headaches, stomach cramps, sweating, muscle tension, aches in the neck or lower back. The body can act as an indicator of a variety of emotions – fear, anger, frustration, boredom, lethargy, depression, excitement and guilt can all be physical as well as emotional and intellectual experiences. The person in need can be helped to recognize the link between their body states and their own thoughts and feelings as a part of the helping process. In addition, the body itself is the source of a great deal of unhappiness and distress amongst those seeking help. For example, there are certain social conditions which express themselves bodily – anorexia (prolonged loss of appetite) and obesity being just two that come to mind immediately. Young people and elderly people are very conscious of body image – so much so that their social behaviour is affected by negative body images. A great many single people who seek partners but find relationships difficult to sustain suggest that their body image is the crucial variable making all the difference to their success.

These introductory remarks suggest that the counsellor or helper needs to be aware of the extent to which the body can be an indicator of difficulties experienced by the person in need or a source of presenting problems. In addition, the helper ought to consider carefully the extent to which the body can be the focus for helping activity, through the use of relaxation training, massage and meditation.

In this chapter three aspects of the body's place in helping – as an *indicator*, as a *source* and as a *focus* – will be examined, and practical helping activities will be suggested. Special attention is paid to the link between body and feeling states, with activities being suggested that may assist the helper in meeting the needs of the person they are helping.

Other chapters have mentioned the importance of the helper giving attention to the body and its needs during the course of a helping relationship. For example, when examining the task of the helper seeking to restore active coping, Chapter 4 suggested that helpers and counsellors need to attend to the physical condition of those they are seeking to help (especially if they are in crisis). A person in poor physical shape often finds new tasks and challenges more difficult to undertake than those who are in better health. The chapter dealing with feeling-focused helping (Chapter 7) also mentions that the way a person talks about feelings is sometimes matched by a body action which the helper might wish to draw attention to or exaggerate. Dreamwork is physically active – it involves re-enactment – because the person is seen to experience emotions intellectually and physically. I now draw these strands together and remind you to look at the person with the same intensity as you listen to them, since the body often suggests that the verbal statements being made by the person are only a part of their story.

A word of caution. There are many books about non-verbal behaviour available – books like *Manwatching* and *Intimate Behaviour* by Desmond Morris. These suggest that particular gestures or postures are indicative of particular emotional states. For example, sitting upright with arms folded in front of the chest suggests defensiveness and is most often contrasted with the person sitting in a relaxed style with legs open and arms outstretched, which is said to be a position of openness. Though Morris provides a useful starting point for thinking about physical movements and positions, it is often not possible to interpret the meaning of a gesture simply through an observation. The helper needs to avoid over-interpretation of body movement and needs to be mindful of the fact that gestures and styles of sitting and reacting are both learned and rooted in culture. So treat books about non-verbal behaviour which seek to offer standardized interpretations of gestures and postures with caution. They are intended to encourage you to consider the link between physical gestures and posture and emotional/intellectual activity and are not accurate diagnostic sources.

A further caution along the same lines. Many books about stress and anxiety strongly recommend the use of relaxation as a means of reducing stress and anxiety levels. Yet several studies have shown that some people find relaxation training stressful in itself! This is especially true of those whose stress can be seen to derive from bore-dom and who prefer high rather than low activity levels. Training someone to relax as a way of coping with stress is therefore useful for some people and not for others. This is also true for meditative techniques and massage. The point being made here is simple: there are few generalizable rules about either the meaning of gestures or the effectiveness of body-focused helping. You have a major task in establishing the meaning the person attributes to their own body images and movements and the extent to which these attributions are a source or an indication of their difficulty. You will also need to establish clearly the purposes and likely outcomes of body-focused helping techniques before using them with anyone, espe-cially if the person is reluctant to see their body as a means for changing the way they think and feel.

The body as indicator

Imagine two people. Glyn is unhappy and depressed and feels that all those around him are well and energetic. He loses weight and has little energy. He feels tense, so much so that he aches in muscles he uses regularly. He finds a nervous tick in his left eye that he had as a child has returned. He sweats more than usual and has several headaches during a typical working week. He slumps in his chair at work and home, and drinks to dull his feelings.

Terry is depressed and feels that all those around him are also depressed and unhappy. He avoids eye contact with these other peo-ple (who also avoid eye contact with him). He sleeps badly and has lost his appetite – he has no energy. He slumps in his chair and feels and looks deflated. He is slow in his movement and his speech. Others avoid walking with him because he is so slow. In the cases of both Glyn and Terry their physical posture and behaviour are indicative of their emotional state. Terry appears more depressed than Glyn and neither of them eats or sleeps well. Both are acutely conscious that their bodies and their behaviour 'give the game away' as far as their emotional state is concerned. Even if people do not know why Glyn and Terry are depressed they certainly know that they are depressed – it shows itself in a variety of ways. In both these cases the body is an indicator of the unhappiness and depression the person feels.

The body also reflects feelings of energy and activation, or excite-ment and pleasure. Reaction times and alertness are better when you feel confident rather than stressed; an excited person shows their high energy through their eyes and their speech – sometimes their speech runs away with them and they jumble and confuse words because they are so excited. The body is an indicator of what some psychologists have called 'emotional tone' – the over-riding tone or mood of the emotions a person feels at a particular moment.

Since moods and emotional states can change quickly, the body can be used as an indicator of change. Under certain conditions of stress, some individuals produce small pouches under the eye that appear and disappear within a moment. Others produce higher heart rates which appear and then dissipate quickly. A variety of measuring devices have been developed which are commercially available to monitor changes in heart-rate, respiratory rate and skin temperature. The use of such devices is common in the practice of *biofeedback* – a practice described more fully later (page 106).

Though the body can show changes in mood and temperament that take place over relatively short periods of time, there is a need to understand that the body is also displaying a consistency in behaviour over time. For example, some individuals are more morning persons than evening persons ('larks') whilst others are more active and live in the evenings than in the mornings ('owls'). Other studies suggest that there is a clear group whose behaviour is characterized by speed and impatience, competitiveness and hard-driving and high levels of job involvement. This group, known as Type A persons, are contrasted with those who take life as it comes, who are moderate in their behaviour and who seek to do their best under a variety of conditions (Type B persons). Type A persons are characterized by certain behavioural features: they eat quickly, they walk speedily, they interrupt those who take time coming to the point in conversation, they bring work home with them and are impatient when others are late for meetings. This kind of behaviour makes special demands on the heart and cardio-vascular system; so much so that several studies suggest that the Type A person is much more at risk of heart disease than those who are Type B and do not behave in this way. This example of behaviour indicating possible proneness to illness shows clearly how the body can be an indicator of a possible future problem.

These points make clear that the body can be regarded as an indicator of:

- the current emotional state of the person
- the extent to which the person's emotional state is changing during the course of a particular encounter

- possible future difficulties which the person might experience.

The helper's task is to attend to body postures and actions with these points in mind. In particular, by using the technique of mirroring the helper can draw the attention of the person to the way in which their body reflects their emotions. This involves the helper 'playing back' the physical posture or movements they have seen the person use and asking them to explain what these movements or postures mean to them. By further exaggerating the movements or postures, the helper is able to examine with the person in need the impact their body has upon their behaviour, thoughts and feelings. Often the person in need is unaware that their body shows others (more clearly than their words) just how they feel.

An alternative technique can be used when the person shows little awareness of their body movements and postures being linked to their emotions. When a person says they are depressed or excited they can be asked by the helper to show what these emotions look like without using words. They can be asked to exaggerate the physical features of these emotions and then show the extent to which they actually feel depressed or excited (or whatever emotion is under discussion). A person who is not fully aware of their body and its 'language' will find this activity difficult and yet rewarding. For it begins to show them that they can affect their emotional state by the way that they behave. This technique is sometimes called picturing – since the non-verbal display of emotions presents a picture of an emotional experience. Helpers with access to video recording facilities will find the recording and replaying of such picturing activity a powerful way of drawing the person's attention to the link between the body and feelings.

When the helper wishes to draw attention to the extent to which the person's emotional state can be seen to change during the course of an encounter they need either to reflect on such changes by summarizing what they have seen or they need to make use of some of the instrumentation available that records these changes. It is possible to buy a small machine which produces a sound (usually a buzz) whenever the temperature of a person's skin surface changes. These machines are used in association with relaxation training activities. Typically, a person is asked to attach a small plasticated ring to their index finger and this ring is connected by a small wire to a machine about the size of a pocket radio. Whenever the skin temperature increases a small buzzer sounds – this occurs because such an increase is seen to be associated with anxiety. Whenever a decrease occurs or the temperature is stable then there is no sound. The helper talks the person through a situation which they find anxiety provoking or gets them to experience that situation directly. Each time the buzzer sounds, they teach the person to relax and begin the process again. Because the person has some audio-feedback on the extent to which they are able to control their anxiety through relaxation it is thought that they will develop skills to control their level of bodily anxiety and, in so doing, reduce their anxiety levels generally. This process of teaching people to relax whenever they begin to feel anxious using an auditory stimulus to show them that they are beginning to feel anxious is known as *biofeedback* and is a widely used form of self-regulation of the emotions.

So far in this section I have mentioned some techniques intended to draw the person's attention to the way in which their bodies reflect their underlying emotional state. In addition I have looked briefly at a particular method for reducing anxiety – biofeedback – in order to demonstrate that counselling and helping can involve the direct use of body measurement as a basis for helping work. We now need to elaborate these ideas in the context of some broader understanding of the link between the body as indicator and the nature of a person's psychological well-being.

A great many of the psycho-physiological problems which a person experiences can be seen to relate to:

- the failure of the person to release psychological and physical tension
- the desire of the person to repress psychological conflicts within themselves
- the person's attempt to inhibit the expression of undesirable thoughts or emotions – the inhibition of painful self-talk
- the desire to receive and maintain attention through the development of physical symptoms – being physically ill often draws more attention and expressions of emotional support than expressing unhappiness or depression
- the experience of intolerable levels of stress from events that the person was unable to anticipate or felt unable to control.

You as helper need to decide which one of these five categories is the most appropriate for understanding the physical indications the person is showing for some psychological distress or disturbance. The tactics you use to help the person deal with the physical and psychological aspects of their difficulties will critically depend upon your hypothesis. The five listed above are the most frequently called upon hypotheses when the helper feels that the physical state of the person indicates some underlying disturbance. Biofeedback is appropriate when the helper feels that the physical features of the person's present problem arise out of a need to learn to cope better with the physical consequences of stress or anxiety.

The body as a source of presenting problems

So the helper may need to see the body as an indicator of underlying psychological problems – it provides a 'clue' to some underlying psychological need which the person is expressing. But there are also a number of situations in which the person in need seeks help because of direct concerns about their body. These include:

- the person who is experiencing anorexia or bulimia
- the person who feels that they are over-weight but yet feels unable to lose weight
- the person who feels that they are addicted to some substance which they wish they were not addicted to – alcohol, minor tranquillizers, cigarettes, toxic glue
- the person experiencing genuine physical pain who is seeking psychological ways of reducing that pain.

The helper needs to develop the skill of distinguishing between the person who presents some physical feature of their self as an indicator of a deeper psychological need and the person who, though they may have deeper psychological needs, has a significant physical problem.

This may seem a rather fine distinction to make. But it is a practical distinction. It is rather like the distinction between the person who *thinks* that they might fail an examination and the person who *has* failed an examination: both have a focus on consequences but for one the nature and intensity of the consequences are more substantial than for the other. In the case of the body as a source of a person's presenting problem the helper has to deal directly with both the physical *and* the psychological difficulties the person is experiencing.

The first practical step a helper should take is to ensure that they are fully aware of the current local medical opinion concerning the problem they are dealing with. For example, a person who wants to reduce or end their dependence upon minor tranquillizers is clearly being prescribed these tranquillizers by a medical practitioner. What is the predominant opinion of medical workers in the area about the nature of tranquillizer addiction and the ways in which this addiction can be reduced? Simply by posing this question I make clear that the helper seeking to work in this field needs to have very close and direct contact with a medical practitioner if they are to find themselves in conflict with local medical opinion. Indeed, in many cases they will need to collaborate with a medical practitioner if they wish to be effective.

The second question concerns the level of the helper's understanding of the medical or physical phenomena with which they are dealing. The various organizations concerned with helping people overcome their physical difficulties – for example, Weightwatchers, Alcoholics Anonymous – provide detailed guides to the difficulties an individual will experience in seeking to change their physical condition. Helpers should familiarize themselves with the appropriate materials and information from these sources.

The third question I think it appropriate for a helper to ask is: 'What can I do better than the organizations devoted to the specific care of the persons with a specific presenting problem?' (for example, alcoholism, glue-sniffing, over-dependency on minor tranquillizers). In many cases the answer will be 'very little'. The most useful thing the helper can do under these circumstances is to encourage and enable the person to make and keep contact with the organization appropriate for their condition. There is no sense in a helper seeking to achieve the same results as a local agency with expertise and several years of proven competence – the task thus becomes one of making a sensitive referral to the agency concerned and continuing to offer support to the person once the referral has been effected.

Should the helper decide to maintain the primary helping role with a person with physical problems then they need to ensure that their helping strategy does not add to the physical problems which the person faces. For example, if the person is reporting high levels of pain and the helper is seeking to reduce these through psychological means the helper may suggest relaxation exercises of some kind. Some of these exercises involve the tensing of muscle groups which, if practised on a regular basis, could conceivably add to the person's difficulties rather than reduce them. Psychologists generally engage in such counselling only with appropriate medical supervision.

So my own view is to regard this category of presenting problem as deserving of a response by a helper with skills and experience in dealing with the specific presenting issue. In fact, a useful guideline to adopt is: if you are not sure, refer. There is a network in Britain and in other countries of skilled clinical and counselling psychologists who are trained and supported to work with just this kind of difficulty and it seems to me appropriate that this network should be used to the full.

The body as a focus for helping

Before detailing ways of using the body as the prime method of helping a person, it is necessary to address an ethical question. You will recall that earlier (Chapter 3) it was suggested that the person seeking help expects their helper to behave ethically. Some of those who seek help will not accept physical methods of helping as ethical. For example, the use of massage is an established way of reducing direct feelings of tension and stress; for it to be effective, the person in need will need to undress (though not completely) – many find this unacceptable. The helper therefore needs to ensure that their intentions are clear to those they are helping and that they accept these methods as appropriate to their needs. Furthermore, the helper needs to be aware that the use of methods involving high levels of physical contact will also raise issues for the helper about the degree of risks they take, for example when they massage a member of the opposite sex. Some organizations do not encourage (indeed, forbid) their helpers to engage in physical ways of helping – the helper therefore needs to consider their appropriateness both to the person in need and to the organization for which they work. Finally there is a need to recognize that helping through the body is more acceptable in some settings than in others – there is a need for privacy and for respect to be shown to the needs of the person. These ethical issues may or may not arise in your own circumstances, but it is appropriate to remind you of them here.

Relaxation training

Relaxation training is used for a variety of difficulties which those in need present. Most commonly it is used to reduce the effects of daily stress and to overcome the physical impact of periods of high physical activity. Additionally, relaxation training has been used effectively with high blood pressure, migraine, insomnia and asthma.

Relaxation training usually involves several different components and it can take between four and 10 hours of helper training time for the person to learn to use relaxation methods to effectively self-regulate their own stress. The person in need is given a set of instructions asking them to relax. They assume a passive and relaxed position, usually lying down with the neck supported by a small cushion. A quiet atmosphere and privacy is essential to effective relaxation. The person is then asked to breathe deeply, pressing all the air out of their lungs slowly before the fresh intake of breath. At the same time they are asked to concentrate on their breathing and to 'let go' of mental images and concerns which relate to the stress they are experiencing. If the person has difficulty in letting go, the helper can offer them a pleasant scene to focus upon, such as a sunny day by a riverbank, and ask them to concentrate upon this scene to the exclusion of other thoughts. They are asked to tense and relax muscles in their body in a particular sequence (described below) so that they can directly experience the difference between tension and relaxation. Through their experience of this switching between tension and relaxation the person is enabled to understand the physical means by which they can relax and they can then develop the skill of relaxing quickly. To be effective, relaxation training should be practised daily without supervision for about 25 minutes for about one month.

There are various relaxation techniques which the helper can use. These include long and complex procedures as well as short and simple ones. The procedure I use and prefer is as follows.

Having got the person comfortable and relaxed and having checked that they are breathing deeply I begin this pre-training sequence:

- gradually close your eyes (6–7 seconds)
- tense (30 seconds) and then relax (1 minute) your left forearm
- tense (30 seconds) and then relax (1 minute) the whole of your left arm
- tense (30 seconds) and relax (1 minute) the whole of your left arm again
- tense (30 seconds) and relax (1 minute) your right forearm
- tense (30 seconds) and relax (1 minute) the whole of your right arm
- tense (30 seconds) and relax (1 minute) the whole of your right arm again.

Then I say that the relaxation training procedure will involve them in tensing particular muscles for about 30–40 seconds and then relaxing these muscles for about 50–60 seconds. Each time they tense muscles they are to attend to *exactly* what this feels like – they are asked to imagine what the muscle is doing, what it must look like and what colour it must be. When they then relax these muscles they are asked to imagine these same things – what is happening to the muscles, what must it look like, what colour is it? Having done this pre-activity exercise they are now ready for relaxation training proper. The complete activity is as follows:

1. Bend your left hand back at the wrist, maintaining the pressure at the bend for about 40 seconds – imagine what it looks like and notice the tension in your wrist.

2. Now let that hand relax, let all the tension flow from the hand – attend to the difference between it being tense and now relaxed, what must the muscle look like, what colour is it, what does it feel like right now? (You do not want the person to answer these questions but to think about them and consider them – it is a device for changing their thoughts from stress to relaxation.)

3. Repeat steps 1 and 2.

4. Now bend the arm at the elbow and hold it there for around 40 seconds – notice the tension and imagine the muscle.

5. Now relax the arm as much as you can – just feel the tension flowing out of the arm.

6. Repeat steps 4 and 5.

7. Now raise the left arm as high as you can from the shoulder – push it up into the air and clench your fist so that all the muscles in this arm are tense and taut – hold it there for 50 seconds, concentrating on the feeling of those muscles as tense.

8. Now relax the left arm as completely as you can – feel the muscle tension leave you and feel those muscles relaxing and becoming warm again, just feel the difference between tension and relaxation.

9. Repeat steps 7 and 8.

10. Now undertake the same steps with the right arm (steps 7–9).

11. Now bend your left foot back towards your left knee as far as you can and hold that foot in this tense position for 40 seconds, paying attention to the tension and the tautness of the muscles in your foot.

12. Now relax all the muscles in your foot.

13. Repeat steps 11 and 12.

14. Now bend your left leg at the knee so that all the muscles above and below the knee feel taut and tense – notice this tension and feel the muscle become tight and taut.

15. Now relax the left leg and feel the tension easing out of the muscles and the leg becoming relaxed.

16. Repeat this process (steps 14–16) with the right leg.

This is usually enough to establish the principles of relaxation training. The remainder of this listing simply states the muscle group which the helper will need to tense and relax for the complete programme.

17. Neck and shoulders – try to make your shoulders touch your ears.
18. Forehead – wrinkle the forehead and try to imagine all the creases.
19. Nose and mouth – wrinkle the nose, press the lips together.
20. Eyes – close your eyes as tightly as you can.
21. Abdominal muscles – draw them in as if expecting a punch.
22. Genitals – tense and relax all the muscles you can find down there.

Throughout this activity, the helper needs to speak in a calm and even voice and pay very careful attention to the person's physical posture. If they look at all in pain, then it is time to issue the relax instruction. The full routine as outlined here takes approximately 40–45 minutes to complete and should take this time if the muscle tensing is to be effective and if adequate time is to be given to the muscles to relax. The aim of subsequent training sessions is to increase the speed at which the person is able to tense and then relax these muscles. It is important that the person practises these activities on their own as a 'homework' assignment – they have to aim to make the tensing and relaxing of their muscles something that they can achieve at will anywhere. As the sessions progress and the person is able to achieve bodily relaxation in a very short time (say 10 to 15 minutes) then the helper will want to discuss with the person the way in which they ought to use what they have learned to modify their responses to stress when this occurs. In particular, the helper can emphasize that whenever the person feels their body becoming tense they ought to respond in the way that they have now been taught and relax the appropriate muscles.

It should be clear that this process is a demanding one for both the helper and the person in need – it requires a great deal of concentration and a considerable investment in time. In addition, not all those who experience stress will find this process helpful. Though there are some shorter relaxation programmes available, most require the person to practise and develop the skill of relaxing quickly over several hours of work. Many get frustrated by the time it takes to learn the relaxation response and others regard such a physical response to emotional stress as inappropriate to their psychological needs. Nonetheless, relaxation training is a valuable adjunct to other counselling and helping strategies and is often effective as a stand-alone method of helping.

Meditation

There are two basic forms of meditation – passive and dynamic. In passive meditation the person is asked to find a place where they can be quiet and relax so that they can focus upon an idea (or *mantra*) to which they intend to give their full attention. The nature of a mantra varies with the particular school of passive meditation being followed. My own favourites for use in helping are 'concentrate on the sound a bird might make in flight' and 'imagine the sounds fish make in water'. The idea is to concentrate upon these thoughts to the exclusion of all others. This process of deep concentration requires the person to give attention to this thought with all of their body and mind – the thought has to be all-embracing, any bodily sounds produced by the person who is meditating are examined and explored to see if they illuminate the mantra in any way. To be effective, the person has to be encouraged to relax (see previous section) and develop the skill of concentrating upon their mantra to the exclusion of everything else. The helper can assist the person in need by showing them how to relax and by developing with that person a mantra that helps them meditate quickly. The purpose of such a meditative exercise is to provide a device by which the person can substitute thoughts about the mantra whenever they begin to experience stress.

In contrast, dynamic meditation is physically active and exhausting. Developed by the followers of Bhagwan Shree Rajneesh (a guru), dynamic meditation involves the person in four sequences of physical movement. In the first sequence (lasting 15 minutes) the person is asked to shake themselves as much as they can – they shake their arms and legs and their bodies in any rhythm that feels right to them. What matters is that they shake and concentrate on shaking. In the next sequence (also for 15 minutes) they dance and enjoy the movement of the dance – how they dance does not matter as long as they dance. In the third sequence they relax completely by simply lying down or sitting with their eyes closed and focusing upon what it feels like to be relaxed. This third phase also lasts for 15 minutes. In the final phase they gradually move from the reverie of relaxation to the reality of the room in which they are present, moving slowly and deliberately until they 'pick up' the speed of normal life. All of this is done to the accompaniment of music. The first sequence of the music is rapid and rhythmic, providing a tempo by which the person can shake themselves; the second segment also needs to be rhythmic but can vary its rhythms to provide variety in the dance sequence; the third musical segment needs to be soft and tranquil, as also does the fourth. The Rajneesh Foundation supply specific tapes for this purpose, but it is possible for helpers to develop their own. The important feature of the music is that it provides a broad and general framework for the meditation exercise. In the course of this activity, the person will find that their concentration shifts from the task of performing to the helper's satisfaction to simply being involved in the dancing and movement to the point at which they are completely in touch with their thoughts and feelings, all of which are focused upon the movements of the body. It is an effective way of losing oneself in one's body and of emptying the mind of the stress and anxiety which the person has brought to such an activity. It is a meditation exercise precisely because the person loses the social self in the inner self. It is effective because of the way in which deep concentration can be achieved.

I have used dynamic meditation with teachers, doctors, nurses, social workers, lawyers and many other groups. What is most interesting is that almost all have reported that they were able to experience a psychological and physical change during the course of the hour that this activity takes. In addition, the repeated use of this procedure on a daily basis for up to one month has led some of those with whom I have worked to claim that dynamic meditation was a kind of indoor jogging and relaxation training combined. After a week or so of practice, these individuals reported that they could reduce their stress at the office or in relationships by remembering the experience of dynamic meditation.

In both forms of meditation it is important that the helper introduce the person to the activity carefully. The helper also needs to be mindful of the physical nature of dynamic meditation – those who are physically unwell or who have a history of cardio-vascular disease should not be encouraged to undertake this form of meditation.

Massage

Massage is rarely used in helping relationships since it involves the person in need undressing completely or almost completely and is an intimate contact between the helper and the person seeking help. In addition, massage is not a technique that has been well researched in terms of its efficacy in reducing stress. Whilst those who practise massage claim that it is effective in reducing stress and tension directly, it is not clear whether massage can in any way affect the extent to which the person subsequently experiences stress.

Briefly, the practice involves the helper in relaxing the person in need (see above) and applying rhythmic pressure to the muscles of the neck, back, hips, legs, chest and face such that the pressure tenses the muscles which then relax. The massaging of a person is helping if:

- the helper has warm hands and does not lose physical contact with the person during the course of the massage – one hand should remain on the person's body throughout the massage process
- a massage oil is used to lubricate the hands of the helper so as to minimize skin friction
- the temperature of the room in which massage takes place is sufficiently warm for the person to remain wholly or partially undressed for the duration of the massage
- throughout the massage process the helper talks gently to the client, encouraging them to relax.

Massage can also be a valuable vehicle for a guided fantasy in which the helper takes the person in need through the situations which they have been experiencing as stressful and encourages them to imagine themselves as un-stressed in these same situations. By combining massage with such a fantasy the person can be encouraged to associate non-stressful self-talk with pleasant experiences (few suggest that massage is unpleasant!), and can so develop their coping repertoire.

Should you wish to develop massage as a vehicle for helping then you should look at the various massage books available in bookstores. There are so many that it is hard to make a specific recommendation, though I have listed one at the end of this chapter which I have found especially useful.

The body is a neglected feature of the person who seeks help. Any organization which seeks to help people with stress and anxiety needs to accept that the body is a vehicle by which stress can be reduced and needs to explore the use of relaxation training, meditation, massage and other physical activities which can reduce stress in the short and long-term. Helpers wishing to use these methods, provided that they are mindful of the ethical issues they sometimes give rise to, should be encouraged to develop their skills and abilities.

Suggested reading

Jacobson, J. (1938) *Progressive Relaxation*. Chicago: Chicago University Press.
The original source of most contemporary relaxation training programmes and, despite its age, still well worth reading in detail. It contains routines and programmes and suggestions for their use.

Carrington, P. (1977) *Freedom in Meditation*. New York: Doubleday/Anchor.
An introduction to the philosophy and practice of meditation. A useful starting point from which to learn more about meditative techniques and schools of meditation.

Downing, G. (1982 edition) *The Massage Book*. Harmondsworth: Penguin.
A practical and detailed guide (with illustrations) to massage. It includes suggestions about what to massage when, how to massage and what oils are helpful. Cheap and invaluable.

Chapter 9

Helping the Helper

The first eight chapters of this book have outlined a variety of roles, strategies and tactics which a helper or counsellor can use when they seek to help a person in need. The strategies range from helping a person in crisis through to helping a person examine the significance a dream has for them. In addition, the relationship between helping and teaching has been explored in the context of social skills training. In reading these chapters you may have noticed a repeated emphasis on the helper making a clear contract with the person they are helping so as to set limits or boundaries around those things the helper is willing to do. Also, there has been an emphasis on the need for the helper to regard the various strategies and tactics outlined here as a part of an ongoing helping relationship in which their needs as a helper are as important as the needs of the person they are helping. Finally, there is a repeated suggestion that the helper needs to be mindful of the consequences of the helping process for the person that they are helping *and for themselves.*

I now look at ways in which counsellors and helpers can help themselves. This issue is included because it is important for helpers to avoid becoming so routinized that all semblance of spontaneity and genuineness has gone from their work. It is also important that helpers understand the importance of their own need for support and supervision as a feature of their helping.

Being a helper – some limits

When a person seeks your help they expect you to be able to display warmth, genuineness and empathy with their situation and their thoughts and feelings. They expect you to be in command of your own thoughts and feelings, so that you are clear in your understanding of their needs and direct in your response to these needs. They also expect that you are going to be competent in the skills you employ. They *don't* expect you to have difficulty in grasping the points that they are making or in seeing a way of helping them. What is more, many of those looking for help expect it to be a relatively quick process.

Another way of expressing these observations is that the person in need expects you to be: *alert, attentive, supportive, competent, incisive, decisive, direct,* and *successful* – all in a short time! Now these are laudable ideals to hold for a helper. Were I to be seeking your help I would hope that these descriptions would be appropriate to both you and the help you offered me. But we have seen earlier (Chapter 6) that holding the view that a person (such as a helper) should be thoroughly competent and achieving in all the things that they do at all times is irrational. Whilst it would be nice to think that you could be such an ideal helper, in reality you are going to have 'off days' and periods of not 'getting it together' as a helper. It is only rational to expect that a helper will have strengths and weaknesses, good and bad days, successes and failures, blind-spots, idiosyncrasies and passions. If they did not they would not be human and frail.

Being a helper is a task that carries many opportunities for being human and frail. When the person you are helping is experiencing a deep grief from the recent loss of her husband or child, a helper will feel their own emotions being pulled out and bared. This situation encourages the helper to think of their own relatives and family members and asks them to address the question: how well will I cope with the loss of one or more of these people? When the person you are helping is examining the impact of becoming unemployed after feeling themselves to be in a secure position for 11 years, it is natural that this makes the helper consider their own job security. In contrast, helpers can share moments of real joy and discovery with those that they help, and enjoy many opportunities to provide support, comfort and emotional comradeship. It is because a helper is both human and frail that they are able to empathize and understand and help another, frail human being.

The ability of the helper to help effectively will be impaired by a variety of conditions. For example, many of those who provide counselling and helping services do so either as part of some other work (for example, nurses, teachers, dental assistants, social workers) or on a voluntary basis. Often the time available to them for the task of helping or counselling is inadequate; plans made on one day have to be changed on another because of changes in work arrangements; there is a lack of security in voluntary work that often makes it difficult for a helper to sustain a long-term helping relationship. These variables about the *structure* of the helping situation can affect the ability of the helper to provide a service which he or she feels comfortable with. Then there are the helper's own *emotional* needs that affect the helping relationship – imagine trying to help someone on the day before you are due to move house, or on the day that your daughter or son has been taken to hospital with a broken arm; or helping a person who is coping with cancer a few days after your mother or father has been told that they have the disease. The helper's own vulnerability, whilst showing them to be human and fallible, impairs their efficiency as a helper. There are also impairments which arise from the content of the needs which a person in need presents. For example, if you are a female helper who has recently received a series of obscene phone calls which you have found difficult to cope with, will your ability to handle the sexual fetish of a person in need be affected in any way? Alternatively, there are some helpers who do remarkably good work, but have certain blind spots – death, sex, violence and addiction are sometimes regarded as 'difficult' areas for many of those who do valuable voluntary work as helpers.

These points about structure, the helper's emotional needs and the blind spots a helper might have suggest that the helper ought to develop a clear understanding of their own limitations. The helper should also attend to the way in which their needs interact with those of the people they are seeking to help. This is important if the helper is to retain confidence in their own work and if some of the excesses which can and do arise are to be avoided (see Chapter 3).

One way of assessing the limits to your work is to keep a brief progress diary in which you list the strengths and weaknesses you feel you have in relation to each of the individuals you are helping. This need not be a long and detailed document – the shorter and more succinct the better. But it is a way of recording both what you see as happening and, over time, your development as a helper. In addition, the diary may help show you a pattern to your work – for example, what kind of person you are feeling confident about helping, whether you are more confident after some event (such as a training event or a period of reflection), or whether you seek support from others about particular kinds of problem.

Another way of assessing your limits is to seek a regular meeting with *another helper* so as to explore what is happening to *you* as a helper. You use your time with this helper as a way of looking at and reflecting upon your work in a way that is helpful to you – it is a form of diary keeping with the additional benefit that the diary will talk back and ask you questions or ask you to elaborate.

A final way of assessing your own limits as a helper is to tape record or video a series of sessions with a person and offer yourself a critique of them. In doing so be sure to seek the permission of the person you are helping, making clear to them that the tapes are for your own use and will not be shown or listened to by others. Should you decide to do this there are two questions which you should ask yourself throughout the time you are listening to the tape. These are: '*what* is happening right now?', and *how* does whatever is happening come to be happening – how can I describe this by reference to my own actions as a helper? These questions will illuminate the process of helping that you are using and enable you to recall the situation you were in and the thoughts you had about it as it was happening. They also enable you to avoid asking the question you might think is the most useful, namely 'was this good or bad?'.

Experience of training helpers in counselling and helping skills in several countries has taught me that the 'what' and 'how' questions listed here produce more learning and more development than the 'good or bad' question. What this evaluation process subsequently does is to provide the person who seeks to help others with the ability to ask themselves the 'what' and 'how' questions when the helping is actually taking place. Indeed, using tapes and video material in this way increases the ability of the helper to reflect upon the helping process when it is actually happening and facilitates detailed recall of thoughts and ideas when the helper later tries to recall the helping process. Be warned: this process takes a considerable amount of time and often produces some discomfort on the part of the helper, since tactics which 'felt' good at the time often do not look or sound so good after a few hours have passed. But do not be deterred by this warning (or the technical difficulties associated with recording). The use of recording devices for self-assessment and development is a long-established vehicle for self-development in counselling and helping, and is regarded as an effective method of exploring the limits to a person's helping abilities.

Not all of the limits to helping you might explore in a diary or through the recall process just outlined will relate solely to you. Others will be organizational or situational. For example, I worked as a school counsellor in a school which felt that male counsellors should not see female students unless a third person (preferably an adult, like the school nurse) was also present. I have also worked in a counselling organization that had a policy of 'actively discouraging' its counselling staff from physical contact with those that sought our help. These are intended as clear and explicit limits to the helping that a person can undertake. In both cases I ignored these rules on the grounds that the circumstances demanded some action on my part. Other organizational constraints may not be so explicit. For example, some of the organizations with which I have worked have not addressed the question 'What is a reasonable caseload?', with the consequence that helpers were being asked to carry wholly unreasonable caseloads. The unwritten rule here was that it was a sign of weakness to complain or refuse to accept new cases. The result was that few of those being helped by over-worked helpers were helped to the best of the helper's ability.

Where these organizational rules (explicit or implicit) are encountered as limits to helping then the helper needs to decide whether they ought to help the organization understand itself and develop and change so that the impact of the limitation is reduced or removed. This suggests that helpers often have an educative and consultative role within the organizations for which they work. Whilst there is little scope in a book of this kind to elaborate on this theme, you might usefully bear in mind this thought: an organization devoted to helping people change and develop and overcome difficulties should itself be able to change and develop and overcome difficulties; if the organization is incapable of doing this for itself, how can it claim to be able to do it for others? This provocative thought is the theme of several writings and studies which show that counsellors and helpers working within organizations (such as schools and social work agencies) have a significant role to play in counselling the *organization*. If this is a role you wish to adopt then it is helpful to understand not only your own limits as a helper but the limitations that apply when a person seeks to change or develop an organization from within.

Training

One consequence of identifying a limitation which you feel to be present in your work is to begin to have an agenda for appropriate training. In Britain, training for counselling is extremely difficult to obtain. First, most of the training opportunities that do exist are for teachers as a part of in-service or postgraduate programmes. Second, the provision of training is concentrated in London, though some training programmes are offered at other locations. Thirdly, it is expensive, usually involving significant fees for the completion of diplomas and certificates in counselling.

Since 'counselling' is not a restricted term protected by law in Britain – anyone can establish themselves as a counsellor – there is no real career structure in counselling and the expenditure of a substantial amount of time and money for a professional qualification that is neither needed nor widely used seems somewhat extravagant. Furthermore, though there is an embryo British professional body – The British Association for Counselling (BAC) – it is only recently that training standards and professional accreditation have been determined and there is still considerable uncertainty as to the future of professionalized counselling in Britain. The mere possession of a qualification in counselling is not, however, adequate for professional recognition by BAC.

The National Marriage Guidance Council is the only nationwide counselling organization in Britain that offers a national programme of training. A person is admitted to training following a selection process involving assessment by a panel of experienced counsellors and the taking up of references. Trainees are then put through a training programme aimed at teaching a particular approach to marital counselling based largely on psychoanalytic principles. They undertake counselling under supervision and are able to develop a level of skill through this process which is valuable in other counselling settings. Though some regard the training afforded by the Council to be limited – it concerns itself with marital work and work within a specific framework – the reality is that the Council offers a grounding in counselling and helping across Britain and is the only counselling programme in Britain to offer continued training, support and supervision to its members. Work with the National Marriage Guidance Council is voluntary and its credentials have little academic standing, not that this should deter those of you wishing to receive some basic but invaluable training.

Though these comments about the state of professional training in Britain suggest that the development of counselling as a career might be problematic, there are a variety of opportunities for training throughout Britain, Europe, Canada and America for people with little or no previous experience. These training workshops take a variety of forms and last for anything from one to 20 days. Often they deal with specific features of helping – assertiveness training, interviewing skills, sex therapy, dealing with stress, massage and body work, rational–emotive therapy, and transactional analysis being examples of workshops regularly offered in Britain. The organizations listed at the end of this chapter are usually able to provide details of forthcoming events.

Arrangements for the training and certification of counsellors in Canada, The United States, New Zealand, Australia and Europe differ considerably from the British pattern. On the whole it is expected that the counsellor will be a certified professional who has completed an approved academic programme with predominantly psychological and practical components. Most countries have national organizations for counselling – for example, the Canadian Association for Counselling, the American Association for Counseling and Development and the New Zealand Guidance Association. Such bodies will have details of training programmes and certification procedures for their own country. If in doubt, it is probably best to contact the national psychological society or association or the International Round Table for the Advancement of Counselling.

The quality of training is more important than the certification or accreditation that results from it. For me, training events and workshops are opportunities for learning about other people, about ways of working and about myself. Each new opportunity to participate in an event provides a fresh chance to renew one's resources. There is not a point one can reach as a helper when training is complete, since what is happening in a training event is that the helper is being encouraged to develop as a person. The idea that someone can achieve the status of a *fully* trained counsellor is a contradiction: a counsellor or helper is never fully trained, they are always able to learn more and to develop further.

This last point relates directly to the final point to be made under this heading. The purpose of training is to enable you to develop as a person so that you are able to develop your own style of counselling and helping. There is no 'right way' of helping another person. Consequently, the effectiveness of a helper is very closely related to the extent to which the strategies and tactics they use are genuine to themselves. Counselling and helping are least effective when the helper is simply trying to mimic someone they saw during a training session or to use a tactic they have read about in a textbook but which they do not fully feel is 'right' for them. Thus, when you are involved in a training activity or workshop do not ask 'What do I have to do in order to be like this trainer?' but 'What would it feel like if I were to do that?', or 'Is this really me, or am I simply trying to impersonate someone else?'. The purpose of training is to provide you with an opportunity to learn more about what is possible for you and to aid the development of your personal style. The outcome of training should be enhanced self-reflection and an increased awareness of the possibilities of your own helping skills.

Support and supervision

Training workshops provide opportunities to share ideas and experiences with others as well as being occasions to develop skills and increase awareness. Training events are one means by which a helper or counsellor can obtain support and encouragement from fellow helpers. Such support is an essential feature of the way in which helpers can help themselves. Indeed, a great many experienced counsellors and helpers regularly attend workshops as a way of meeting with colleagues and sharing concerns and insights.

Workshops occur so infrequently in many areas that they cannot reasonably be regarded as an adequate basis for support. For this reason, some counsellors and helpers have created their own support groups and networks. One example is a Consortium of Teachers involved in Pastoral Care and Counselling. This group organizes its own training events and workshops, and has local branches which meet so that those wishing to receive support can do so. A different kind of support scheme is provided by the Care Attendant Support Scheme – a network of those who act as carers for their own seriously ill or disabled relatives and which seeks to provide practical support and respite for those helping their own family in this way. Indeed, many of those engaged in helping and counselling have found their own way of ensuring that they are supported – through talking to friends, colleagues, or family members on a regular basis.

Those wishing to use their support contacts or networks in a more constructive way might wish to conceive of it as more than support but as a vehicle for supervision. The word *supervision* is an unfortunate one – it implies management and control, direction and authority, at least to many people. Here the term is borrowed from psychotherapy, where supervision means guidance and support in a non-directive and mutually beneficial atmosphere. In supervision the helper meets a particular person on a regular basis; in my own case it is monthly, but beginning helpers might feel the need for supervision on a more regular basis. The purpose of these meetings is the mutual sharing of concerns about helping and counselling. To illustrate the nature of supervision, let me describe my own arrangements. The meeting takes two hours. We have agreed on this time-limit since we found that we had a tendency to talk for several hours and we lost the specificity of the meeting. We each agree to occupy one hour of time – at the end of the time we reverse roles. In my time I can ask my 'supervisor' to work in one of three ways:

- Simply to listen to what I have to say – I want to use the time to explore my own thoughts in the presence of another person.
- To listen and interrupt when he is unsure of the meaning of something or when he wishes to seek clarification from me about the implications of the things I am saying.
- I can ask him to push me really hard to make connections between the concerns I have and previous conversations or materials he knows I have read or studied.

These three levels of contract enable me to 'control' my own supervision time. It also ensures that the time is maximally useful to me as a person – I decide what role I wish my supervisor to play since I know best what my concerns are. Most of the time is spent talking about thoughts and feelings I have had about the persons I am trying to help. I concentrate on *what* and *how* questions which I explore through description, role-play or whatever tactic is appropriate to the concern. My aim is to understand the nature of my own helping style and its limitations. At the end of my hour the roles are reversed and I act as supervisor to my colleague who uses the same range of contracts and processes in order to explore his own current concerns.

This description of my own supervision practices involves a particular model of supervision – what is generally referred to as the co-counselling model. There are other models. For example, some organizations ensure that beginning helpers engage in helping in the presence of another person who later offers feedback and comment intended to facilitate the development of the helper's skills. Other organizations, such as the Family Institute in Wales, make use of videos and screens (through which observers can watch a helper work with a person or family without themselves being observed) so that feedback can be provided after (and sometimes during) a counselling or helping session. Yet other forms of supervision involve the work of the counsellor or helper being systematically rated using questionnaires specially designed for this purpose. Here one can provide objective feedback to the counsellor or helper about their behaviour and actions.

Research shows clearly that the quality of helping is enhanced when the person undertaking the counselling or helping role is receiving supervision. This work also suggests strongly that feed-back immediately after actual sessions is the most effective in developing the helper's skills. In addition, the absence of supervision and peer support is seen as a major cause of helper 'burn-out'.

Burn-out – causes and prevention

The term 'burn-out' (derived from the fact that once a rocket has burned-up its fuel it is then useless, but continues to float in space until it crashes) has become gratuitously applied to a great many problems which professional and voluntary helpers and counsellors face. There is nothing inevitable about burn-out: a counsellor or helper can work hard to ensure that they remain sensitive and alive in their counselling and helping sessions and can continue to learn through and enjoy their work after many years of practice. Indeed, regarding counselling and helping as opportunities for the helper or counsellor to learn more about themselves is one way of ensuring that the process of helping retains its interest and value.

Burn-out occurs when the helper or counsellor feels tired, drained and without enthusiasm for a sustained period of time (for example, six months). They feel that the work they are doing is neither appreciated nor effective; that they are not as effective as they once were; that there are too many competing pressures on their time; they feel unappreciated, under-recognized and unimportant; they perform their counselling and helping work as if it were a chore and in a routinized and mechanical way. When looking at their work they find it difficult to recognize any concrete results or achievements. Often they feel oppressed by the organization within which they work. Because they feel so ineffective they are afraid of seeking support and this in turn feeds a feeling of isolation. The result of these features of what many regard as a 'syndrome' is that the helper becomes increasingly ineffective (thereby confirming their own evaluations of their abilities) and disillusioned with their work.

Gerald Corey suggests that there are a number of causes of helper burn-out which the helper needs to understand and anticipate so that it can be prevented. He lists nine causes:

- Doing the same type of helping over and over again with little variation.
- Giving a great deal of one's own emotional and personal energy to others whilst getting little back in return.
- Being under a constant pressure to produce results in a certain time-scale when the time-scale and the pressure are unrealistic.

- Working with a difficult group; for example, those who are highly resistant to change, those who have been 'sent' for help but who do not wish to be helped, or those for whom the chances of change are small because of the nature of their difficulties (for example, the terminally ill).
- The absence of support from immediate colleagues and an abundance of criticism – what might be called 'the atmosphere of certain doubt'.
- Lack of trust between those who engage in helping and those who manage the organizational resources that make helping possible – a feature that is sometimes present in voluntary organizations.
- Not having the opportunity to take new directions, to develop one's own approach or to experiment with new models of working – being unnecessarily constrained.
- Having few opportunities for training, continuing education, supervision or support.
- Unresolved personal conflicts beyond the helping and counselling work which interfere with the helper's ability to be effective, for example, marital problems, health problems.

This is not an exhaustive list – many helpers could add two or three more causes that they feel contributed to their own feelings of frustration which, had they not acted, might have led them to experience burn-out.

Let us illustrate the experience of burn-out by reference to two specific cases.

Mary is a nurse working in a hospice. In recent weeks five of her patients have died and she has also had a death in her own family – an aunt. Mary works hard and is very conscientious. She has recently agreed to participate in a short course offered by the Open University for nurses and to take on extra duties as acting ward sister. She feels overwhelmed by the work she has to do, both at home, in the hospital and for the course. So anxious is she about her work that she is now worried that her anxiety will affect her work – she is anxious about being anxious! The result is that she neglects a particular assignment for one of the patients who then enters a coma. She blames herself for this and seeks permission to return to her normal duties as a nurse, saying 'I am just not up to being given responsibility'. The Nursing Officer, who has training in counselling, recognizes some of the signs of burn-out and develops a counselling programme for Mary based on her accepting responsibility for her own work and learning how to say 'no' without feeling guilty. After three weeks of counselling help, Mary feels more confident about her role as acting ward sister.

Gerry is a social worker. Like all social workers, he carries an unreasonable caseload. In all, he has case officer responsibility for 64 cases. Five weeks ago his Director introduced a new reporting procedure which doubles the workload associated with reporting and documenting contacts with 'clients'. Unlike most of his colleagues, Gerry seeks to implement the new guidelines with a thoroughness and comprehensiveness which is both unnecessary and counter-productive. The result is that Gerry is at the office late each night completing his reports, thereby causing tension at home. Gerry follows through his case work reporting and discovers that none of the case reports he has completed over the last five weeks – about 130 in all – have been read by his area supervisor. What is more, Gerry feels that not only is the procedure worthless but he is worthless. Through counselling and support, Gerry is enabled to see that he is responsible for some of his own stress. He is encouraged to modify his way of thinking about his work through the use of RET techniques.

Avoiding burn-out

Burn-out can be pre-empted or avoided by the helper taking *personal responsibility* for their own well-being. Rather than blaming the 'system' or the 'organization' or the 'lack of local training opportunities', the helper needs to take their own steps to ensure that burn-out is avoided and their helping represents a continued investment in their development as a person. Helpers must own their own feelings and thoughts about what is happening to them rather than blame others or blame systems which they may be unable to affect. Rather than focusing upon what limits them, helpers need to be active in searching for tactics to help themselves avoid burn-out. Some or all of the following may be useful:

- Think of ways of bringing variety into work that one can achieve without seeking the permission of others.
- Take the initiative in starting new projects and not waiting for the 'system' to sanction and approve the steps you take.
- Attend to your own physical health through rest, sleep, diet and exercise.
- Develop new friendships that are characterized by both giving

and receiving.

- Make your own arrangements for your own support and supervision – use the time to develop your own awareness rather than to 'moan' about the 'system'.
- Stop taking on more responsibility for other people's problems – many helpers feel more responsible for the thoughts, feelings and behaviours of those they help than these individuals themselves display.
- Take pleasure in planning your own reading programme about helping – buying this book was a good start!
- Make your own arrangements to attend training and workshop events in your area – if there aren't any, organize some.
- Seek a joint project with a colleague so as to increase the variety of the work that you do.

You need to keep the helping and counselling part of your life in perspective and to cultivate hobbies and interests outside work which are pleasurable in themselves. The thrust of these practical suggestions is that you should take control of your own situation and act so as to feel that you are taking specific steps to maintain your energy and vitality as a person and to continue to learn from your counselling and helping experiences.

Here is a brief description of how Ray, a full-time counsellor, seeks to avoid burn-out:

First of all, I control my workload. I know that I cannot see more than five clients a day and adequately report on my contacts with them. I also know that I am most effective between 8 am and 2 pm and between 6 pm and 9.30 pm. I therefore schedule my client contacts during these times. I do my documentation also during this time, keeping the period 2–6 pm to myself. Usually during this time I will have a brief rest or have a swim. I eat well in the evenings and at breakfast, so I have a light lunch and never miss my meals.

Next I make sure that I talk about my work only to two other people, both of whom I am close with and to whom I can comment about mistakes as well as successes. I also know that I can learn from these people, since they share with me honestly and warmly their own experiences of helping.

Most important: I do not talk about my work with my wife and family (unless something quite extraordinary has happened). My family is a source of activity, interest and amusement to me.

Finally, I pursue my hobby relentlessly ... I collect comedy materials. Tapes, records, videos, joke books ... anything that can give amusement. I also keep a written logbook of jokes I hear – there's a special section on humour in counselling sessions.

This description illustrates that Ray's strategy for avoiding burn-out involves monitoring workloads, resting, having an active interest outside work, not letting work invade other activities, eating regularly and properly and keeping work in perspective.

Maintaining a balanced perspective

Helping can be a demanding and rewarding experience. Because the demands it makes upon us can be considerable we need to keep a close eye on the way we think about some of the basic facets of the helping process. To make this easier for you, I list below some of the facets I keep reminding myself of whenever I have just the beginning of that feeling that 'all is not well ...'.

Facet 1: I can do no more than my best. Whilst we can imagine others being better able to help the person in need (and, indeed, might have suggested this) what I am offering right now is the best that I can offer right now. Though I can always improve on my best, at least I am working at improvement.

Facet 2: Being anxious about my work as a helper is normal. Whilst I might feel concerned or anxious about the work I am engaged in with a particular person at a particular time, such anxiety is both normal and to be expected. Indeed, it is this anxiety that motivates my own learning as a helper.

Facet 3: The helper cannot be perfect. I know it is irrational to think that I must be thoroughly competent and achieving in all the things I do at all times – I cannot be perfect. I can expect to make mistakes. What I wish to be is aware enough to recognize, accept and acknowledge mistakes as they happen and to regard such mistakes as a positive agenda for action on my part.

Facet 4: Instant results are impossible. There are no instant cures for anything. In helping there are no instant cures that I could offer and often I have to wait a long time to see results (if any). What I need to do, rather than look for cures and results, is to understand and be aware of the process I am using so that I can maintain my understanding of *how* I am working and *what* is happening.

Facet 5: I will not succeed with everyone. Few helpers and counsellors have ever claimed that they will be successful in working
with anyone that chooses to seek their help. I am no exception.
I will try to help all those I agree to work with to the best of my
ability and to refer others to the helpers and counsellors I feel are
better able to help them: but I can offer no guarantees.

These five facets of the helping and counselling process are
important reminders of our frailty as helpers. They are intended to
be helpful to the beginning counsellor or helper in showing that
some of the concerns you might have are shared by others with
experience and that the work of helping is inevitably fallible.

Suggested reading

Corey, G. (1982, 2nd edn) *I Never Knew I Had a Choice.* Monterey, Ca.: Brooks
Cole.
Gerald Corey writes excellent counselling and guidance books, most of which are
aimed at professionals and students in training. This book, however, is a self-help
text which seeks to help the reader take greater control of their daily life and seeks
to promote personal responsibility. Highly recommended for all those engaged in
counselling and helping, whatever their qualifications and experience.

Information about training

The following is a brief guide to some of the available information points in English
speaking countries.

BRITAIN
● British Association for Counselling (BAC), 37a Sheep Street, Rugby CV21 3BX,
England.
● Careers Research and Advisory Centre, Bateman Street, Cambridge CB2 1LZ,
England.
● The British Psychological Society (Counselling Psychology Section), St
Andrews House, 48 Princess Road East, Leicester LE1 7DR, England.

CANADA
● Canadian Guidance and Counseling Association, c/o Faculty of Education,
University of Ottawa, 651 Cumberland Street, Ottawa, Ontario K1H 6K9,
Canada.

AMERICA
● American Association for Counseling and Development, 5999 Stevenson
Avenue, Alexandria, Virginia 22304, USA. (Note: This organization used to be
called the American Personnel and Guidance Association.)
● American Psychological Association, 1200 17th Street NW, Washington DC,
Washington 20036, USA.

AUSTRALIA
● Australian Psychological Society (Counselling Section), National Science

Center, 191 Royal Parade, Parkville, Victoria 3052, Australia.

NEW ZEALAND
● New Zealand Psychological Society (Counseling Section), c/o Dept of Education, University of Auckland, Private Bag, Auckland, New Zealand.

INTERNATIONAL
● International Round Table for the Advancement of Counselling, c/o Dr Derek Hope, Brunel University, Uxbridge, England.

Part 3. Helping Contexts

Chapter 10

Helping in Groups

The emphasis so far has been upon a helper working with an individual. Not all counselling and helping takes place in this way. A great deal of counselling activity takes place in groups and in settings in which two or more people are seeking help at a particular time. I now examine the nature of groupwork and the special tasks of the helper who engages in group helping or counselling.

Counsellors or helpers can work with a variety of groups. These range from groups concerned with a specific topic – for example, assertiveness training for women, sexuality, career development or stress – to groups which are non-specific but devoted to personal growth and development. This last type of group, sometimes called a counselling group or an encounter group, can take a variety of forms. It is also important to understand the stages of development in a group and some of the conflicts which can arise in groupwork. The major focus throughout will be upon counselling in groups. Do not see such a specific focus as a limitation: many of the points raised and discussed will be relevant to a variety of groupwork settings. You will need to make links and connections to the groupwork situations with which you are familiar.

The purposes of a group

A helping group can have a variety of purposes. It can be established in order to provide information to participants relevant to some decision a collection of individuals have to make. Alternatively, a group can be formed which intends to use many of the procedures outlined throughout this book in order to effect some specific or general change amongst participants. Finally, a group can be created simply to provide emotional and practical support to participants. One example of an information type group would be a careers information group established so that individuals who wish to change their careers might meet with others who have relevant information. An example of a group intended to change its participants in some way would be Alcoholics Anonymous or Weightwatchers, who have particular targets for behavioural and psychological change for their members. A Women's Aid group meeting regularly to provide support for women who are seeking to develop a better understanding of their own position in the social world is a good example of a support group.

Information, change and support groups function in different ways and involve different kinds of leadership roles for the group leader or helper. For example, a person acting as a facilitator (as the helper or counsellor is usually called in group activities) in an *information*-based group needs to ensure that the information is well and systematically presented, that participants are clear as to the nature and relevance of the available information and that participants have an opportunity to ask questions so that they can better match the information to their needs. In contrast, the facilitator of a *support* group working in a non-directive way will simply seek to create an environment of mutual trust and respect in which all participants feel that it is 'safe' to make statements and examine issues which might be difficult to explore in places other than the group.

It is important in establishing a group to clearly define and specify purposes. For example, there is a considerable difference between attending an information session about widowhood and being asked to disclose one's own experiences of widowhood. Those who are to participate in different kinds of groups need to know just what it is that they are letting themselves in for. Some of the difficulties that arise in groups occur because participants are not as clear as they might be about the function and purpose of a group or about the intended style of working of a group.

The person establishing a group needs to be as explicit as possible about the following questions:

- what is the group's purpose?
- how is it intended that these purposes be achieved?
- who can become a member of the group and how will membership be determined?
- what will be expected of group members – will they be asked to disclose something about themselves or can they be passive?
- under what circumstances can a person end their membership

of a group, and having once left can they later return?

Such questions need to be answered by those who intend to run a group. They are also useful questions to be addressed by those who intend to participate in a group. Only by addressing such questions will the purpose of a group become clear.

Counselling and support groups

Why does a counsellor or helper feel that a group is a useful basis for working? They may feel that a particular individual needs to examine their own way of thinking and feeling about certain issues (for example, sexuality, marriage, parenting) by sharing his or her experiences with others. They will then have an opportunity to examine the different perspectives others bring. Alternatively, the helper may feel that the person needs to develop social skills which can best be achieved through a group-related project. Some people need to belong to a group because they need the support of a variety of people in order to come to terms with some personal experience (such as bereavement or divorce) or some issue (such as sexuality or stress) which is poignant to them.

Group counselling activity can meet all such needs. Clarence Mahler suggests that counselling groups are appropriate for a variety of different needs. They suit individuals who need to:

- Learn to understand others better and the way that others see and understand the social world.
- Learn deeper respect for others, especially others who are different from themselves.
- Develop social skills.
- Experience belongingness through sharing experiences with others – for example, widows, divorcees, women who have been battered by their husbands, sufferers from a debilitating illness.
- Come to terms with certain issues, like sexuality, death, loss, unemployment.
- Benefit from the reactions of others to their views and concerns.
- Engage in individualized counselling and helping work, but prefer to begin their association with helping through a counselling group.

The person establishing a helping and support group needs to be clear which of these reasons are motivating the formation of the group, since this will affect who attends and the style of the group's work.

They also need to address the question: how shall group members be selected? In most cases, counselling and support groups involve some pre-selection interview. For example, in forming a support group for people wishing to give up the use of minor tranquillizers a helper screened those who expressed an interest in terms of: the extent to which they were motivated to attend; their willingness to accept that the group might require them to self-disclose feelings and thoughts which they had not disclosed previously; and the degree to which the person was seen to be able to 'fit in' with other members. Whilst the helper accepts that the selection process was not very scientific or precise, he claims that it was essential to screen out those who might have made the groupwork more difficult and who might have been damaging influences on the other participants. Not all groups involve such pre-selection: where this does not happen some special problems can often develop.

Leadership roles in counselling and support groups

The role to be played by the leader or facilitator in a group is critical in determining how the group works and its effectiveness. There are several features of this leadership role which you might like to consider before establishing a group.

Motivation and philosophy. The first consideration has already been addressed in the previous section – what is the motivation for creating or developing a group in the first place? This involves you as leader making clear to yourself:
- who the group is
- what it hopes to achieve
- why this group is something that you wish to undertake – what are your own motives and likely gains?
- what you have in mind as problems which the group might experience during the course of its development
- how you will evaluate the progress of the group and its success.

Before recruiting the first member, you will need to work through these questions.

In order to work through the questions just listed you will need some philosophy of group process – how do you envisage the group operating and what are the assumptions you are making about the value of personal contributions, the place of self-disclosure, the role of participants as confronters and providers of feedback to others? What role will you have – as initiator, supporter of others, as a director of the group (making sure it 'goes the right way') or as simply a facilitator (letting the group choose its own way of working and its own development)? These questions concern more than the simple mechanics of a group – they are directed at the concept which you hold of the person as a member of a group and the notions of leadership, direction and development with which you intend to work. The questions require you to have a philosophy of groupwork and to make this philosophy explicit to yourself.

Climate setting. Asking questions of yourself about motivation and philosophy is a prerequisite for groupwork. These questions also concern the stage of groupwork that occurs *before* the group meets. Once it does meet there are other concerns that a leader has. The first and most critical is: how can you set the climate of a group? Carl Rogers, the person who developed some of the ideas about the core conditions of helping (see Chapter 2), has addressed this question. He suggests that the core conditions of helping – empathy, warmth, genuineness, immediacy, confrontation, feedback and self-disclosure – are needed just as much in a group setting as they are in working with individuals. He also suggests that the groupworker will need to:

- give direct and personal attention to each of the persons there and show that they are concerned both for the welfare of the group as a whole and for the welfare of individual group members
- establish the parameters of the group by encouraging a group to negotiate a contract about what its concerns are and about how it is to operate
- encourage members to accept each other and validate each other, even when offering feedback or confronting one another. Only in a climate of mutual trust and support can the group develop as a counselling and support group and thereby achieve its aims.

To help the process of climate setting there are a variety of activities and games a leader can use. These 'ice-breaker' activities are intended to promote trust, group cohesion and contact between members. In my own experience they are an artificial but useful way of starting a process by which a group can take increasing responsibility for the work it wishes to do. One of these ice-breaker games involves the leader asking participants to throw a soft cushion at one another – as you receive it you are asked to say your name and in a word or phrase describe how you feel right now. The cushion game is then repeated, but this time the person receiving the cushion is asked to say their name, to thank by name the person who threw the cushion to them and to describe in a few short phrases what they would like the group to do for them and what they are able to offer the group. Such activities ensure that a group can have some fun at its beginning whilst at the same time encourages name recognition and self-disclosure. Such activities thus enable some simple climate setting to be achieved in a relatively short time.

Climate setting is more than the playing of group games. It involves the leader in seeking to actively implement their philosophy of group-based working. What is most critical is that the leader of a group – you – understands that their actions will largely determine the way that the group establishes itself and develops. Thus the leader must display trust and confidence in the group as a whole if they wish the group to work as a whole. They must resist over-planning the life of the group and permit the group to have its own life. They must accept that, whilst they have a specific role in the group, they also are a member of the group and should be subject to the same rules as other members. These points apply even when it is intended that the group leader should 'teach' some skill, such as assertiveness or a communication skill. This needs to be undertaken in a way that shows respect and concern for others and which accepts that the group has its own dynamic, which will affect the quality and nature of the skill teaching.

Problems in leadership. Some of the weaknesses of leader behaviour that occur tell us more about the nature of the leader's role in a group. A common weakness is for the leader to have goals for the group which they do not disclose to the group. For example, they might wish to use the group as a case study of how a group develops over time, but they do not share this goal with the group. This tends to mean that the group feels that there is another agenda at work on occasions but does not know what this agenda might be. The leader should therefore be explicit about their own goals and should encourage others in the group to be explicit about theirs.

A second common weakness in a group occurs when the leader tries to direct a group that is not ready or does not want their direction. For example, the leader might say 'right, we have spent enough time on this work now, let's all ...' when in fact the issues raised by group members need more time to be worked through and need more energy invested in them so that their full value as issues for participants can be realized. Directing a group in a way insensitive to its process and the needs of participants will impair its development.

A third common mistake made by group leaders occurs when they seek to judge the success or failure of a group by the quality of the dramatics that take place within it. For example, one group leader commented that his group 'was a bit weak this time, no one has cried so far'. Groups have their own life and their own dynamics – the dramatics that occur in some groups are a function of the way in which a particular person or group of people choose to express themselves. A group does not need to have dramatics – crying, shouting, leavings, refusals – to be successful. What matters most is the extent to which the group provides an environment in which participants feel able to express themselves and to develop.

A fourth common difficulty which group members experience with leaders occurs when a great deal of the group's time is taken up with leaders exploring their own thoughts and feelings. This is not to say that it is not appropriate for group leaders to disclose what is happening to them as it happens, but it is to say that the leader should be especially conscious that the group is mainly a vehicle for the *participants*, not for him or her.

A further difficulty – the fifth examined here – concerns the leader who offers so many interpretations of the actions of participants (for example, 'You are saying that because ...', 'You saying that is an indication of ...') or of the work of the group (for example, 'This suggests that the group is now primarily concernd with ...' or 'What this tells me about this group is ...') that the group and its members feel that they are a part of some experimental study the leader is conducting on them. Whilst such observations occasionally do bring benefit to the group and its members they do so *because* they occur occasionally. The excessive use of interpretation and comments about the process of the group inhibits its work.

The final and often most critical weakness that group members report when describing poor group leaders is the lack of spontaneity. A group of 12 to 20 people (the usual limit a single group worker is generally willing to work with) requires the group leader to be able to respond sensitively and intuitively to unexpected events. In addition, they wish to feel that this is their group, not just any group – this means that the leader needs to show that they are responding to the people in the room genuinely and spontaneously. The more the leader is seen to be sticking to some well established formula and is using well established lines and routines, the less likely it is that the participants will feel that the leader is being genuine. Genuineness and spontaneity are critical ingredients in the success of groups.

Ethical issues. A section on leadership would not be complete without some reference to the ethical and personal responsibilities of the leader. One of the critical reasons for leadership in a group is to prevent individuals from being damaged by other group members. By 'damage' here I mean both psychological and physical damage. It is important that the leader checks out for signs of participants who are experiencing stress in the group, that he or she establishes contracts about the limits of behaviour in the group and that the leader intervenes whenever they feel that a person is at more risk than is appropriate. These are difficult decisions to make. They involve the helper acting as a leader in the taking of risks. The ability to take such risks comes from experience and a careful working through of the leader's philosophy of groupwork. The best training for leadership is to be an active participant in groups before you begin to lead one. Attend a variety of groups run by others; observe their leadership and discuss with them their philosophy of groupwork; read about groupwork and examine and reflect on your own behaviour as a group member.

Stages of group development

As has been mentioned a few times in the previous sections, groups have their own dynamic – that is, they develop and have a life of their own. Though the speed at which a group develops will vary, depending upon the nature of the group, the quality of leadership and the experience of group members, there are common patterns in the development of groups. To some extent these patterns can be seen as stages of group development. I say 'to some extent' because groups do not always follow these sequences and participants do not necessarily experience the development of a group as a series of steps which build upon each other. Nonetheless, thinking about the development of a group in terms of stages is helpful in illuminating why and how group behaviour can change over time.

Milling around. The first stage of group development is called 'milling around'. People try to get to know each other; they are reluctant to make commitments to each other or to self-disclose; they are simply concerned to make contact. As the group develops, this stage becomes one of resisting personal expression of thoughts and feelings, coupled with a reluctance to explore new thoughts and feelings – participants 'play safe' when asked to describe themselves and their experiences; they look for similarities between themselves and others; they seek to minimize personal risks resulting from self-disclosure. To help participants at these first two stages, the helper needs to show that they accept that the person may experience difficulties and to create a climate in which these difficulties can be overcome.

Describing the past – anecdotal stage. Once some progress has been made in encouraging the participants to disclose more of themselves, they begin by describing past feelings. At this third stage the group's vocabulary is full of 'I used to feel ...' or 'I have often thought ...' or 'Sometimes I feel...but at other times I feel ...'. When this begins to occur it is often helpful for the leader to point to the language used and to suggest some language rules for the group – those discussed in Chapter 7 are usually appropriate.

Negative reactions. When the group begins to speak in terms of the present rather than in terms of the past – the fourth stage of group development – it is most typically through the expression of negative thoughts and feelings. These include negative thoughts about self (for example, 'I will never understand ...' or 'I just can't imagine feeling in any way about ...'), and/or the group (for example, 'Where is all this getting us ...' or 'Look, I came here looking for some answers and all we're doing is talking ...'). The leader might regard these latter comments as reflections upon their own style of working, which in part they are. But it is often necessary for this stage to occur so that the person can unburden their most immediate thoughts and move on to being more open to new ideas and the exploration of feelings. The helper should resist responding to negative comments about the group as if they were some personal attack upon themselves.

Disclosure. Once this negativism phase has been passed through (if it occurs at all) participants seem to free themselves to accept, explore and express personally meaningful material. That is, self-disclosure of inner thoughts and feelings occurs more rapidly and can be encouraged by the leader and other participants with more ease than at previous stages. Such disclosure often leads to the expression of more and more feelings about the group, themselves within the group and about other group members by participants. The leader can be most effective here by validating and accepting comments and encouraging acceptance, feedback and confrontation by other members. In doing so, the leader should be mindful that the group is extremely sensitive and that individuals remain vulnerable as to the extent and nature of the self-disclosures which they regard as beneficial to themselves.

Once the group members accept that self-disclosure leads to confrontation and feedback which they see as constructive (even if painful), then the potential for self-change and development is considerable. At this time there is a cracking of facades and a high level of honesty and personal integrity becomes apparent in groups which are functioning healthily. Also, group members provide considerable support for each other and can take their own steps to heal wounds and reduce pain and increase enjoyment. At this phase the leader needs to be especially sensitive to the risks which individuals take when opening themselves to others and making themselves available for feedback and confrontation. The critical task of the leader is not to rescue an individual experiencing pain but to ensure that the group's overall quality remains supportive and sustaining of its members.

Following the kinds of development just outlined, changes in behaviour, attitudes and patterns of thinking can often occur. This is a good time to teach skills, to share skills and to learn from other participants in the group. The leader can usefully help participants explore the implications of their experience of being in the group for the experience of being in the social world. To some extent, the leader needs to direct the participants to consider the practical and personal consequences of their group experience if the group is to have relevance to the future life of its members. In doing so, the leader needs to be cautious about over-directing the group and about over-generalizing its experience. Each participant will have experienced the group differently – the leader needs to encourage each participant to leave the group with their own personal agenda for action.

So the life of a counselling and support group suggests that the helper needs to examine the progress of the group as a group in just the same way as a parent examines the progress of a child through various stages of development. Throughout, the task of the helper is to nurture the group in its development and act as a sustaining force. Not all groups will develop in this way. Some will need and want more structure; some will move quickly through these various stages. Others will stick at some stages longer than others. The point to note is that groups do have their own developmental pattern and the leader of a group needs to spend time considering the nature of this pattern each time they work with a group.

Making the most of group experiences

One thing the leader can do is to offer some help to participants either before they arrive at a group, or as they arrive, as to how to get the most out of the opportunities a group situation provides for learning. In recent years I have used this list of suggestions for participants as a pre-group briefing:

- Realize that the group is a means to an end, not an end in itself: whilst the group may be important to you, don't lose sight of why you joined and what you intended to gain from your participation.
- You will learn most from this group by trusting yourself to make decisions and by trusting others.
- You are responsible for your own disclosures – decide for yourself just how much you would like to disclose and do not disclose until you are ready to do so.
- You will get most from your involvement in a group by participating in it and least from playing the role of observer – if you wish to benefit become involved.
- A great deal of learning in a group will involve discomfort and sometimes pain – this is normal when you are being asked to critically examine your well established ways of thinking and feeling, so expect this to happen.
- Don't expect the changes that you are looking for to occur quickly and effortlessly in a group – it will take time and may be frustrating, but it is worth persisting.
- Expect to discover things about yourself that you did not know, especially when others start to give you feedback and support.
- You must decide what you do with what you discover and learn – you take the responsibility for using or not using your learning in a group.
- Listen and attend to others as you would wish them to listen and attend to you – be discriminating in your listening and look for the value of other people's talk both for them and for you.
- If you have a persistent feeling (for example, pleasure, frustration, uncertainty, doubt, fear) during a group session, then express it.
- Think for yourself – your needs and your thoughts are what matter to you.

- Pay attention to consistent feedback and decide what to do with it.
- Don't categorize yourself and don't let others categorize you – you are a complex person whom others can only ever partly know, but do listen to the way in which others comment about you, you can learn a lot.
- Don't be afraid to enjoy the experience of discovery and exploration.

Supplying participants with these observations before the group begins presents the group with a basis for a contracting session and ensures that the leader can act to prevent distress by referring to the explicit features of behaviours and relationships documented in this list.

Problems in groupwork

Even the most carefully thought-through philosophy, the systematic selection of participants and the most thorough contracting process will not prevent certain difficulties arising. Though these steps are helpful in minimizing them, a number of difficulties arise simply because of the personality and experience of group participants. In this section nine specific problem behaviours are examined and suggestions for leadership action are made. This is not an exhaustive list, but it provides a basis for thinking about other problems which you may well have experienced.

Silent group members. The first problem is that of non-participating members – individuals who sit on the periphery of the group and choose not to contribute or to respond to developments unless they are pointedly asked to do so. These individuals can disrupt a group in two ways:

- they can give the group the feeling that the group is not a whole group – there are some who are ambivalent about its work
- the attempt to involve this person can distract the group or weaken its work.

Leaders should learn to trust the group to solve such problems. Often the non-participating member will be confronted by the group early in its development and the leader will seek to ensure that such a confrontation is sensitive to the needs of the person. But groups will generally solve this problem in time if left to their own devices.

Monopolizers. The opposite problem, that of a person monopolizing the group, is a more difficult one to resolve. There are several ways a person can monopolize a group – for example, talking a lot, drawing attention to self as a conduit for activities or for support, always seeking to add a comment to comments made by others. The leader can seek to deal with the issue in the group or can wait for the group to learn how to deal with this issue themselves. My own preference is for the latter – the group needs to develop skills in solving its own problems. The more leaders take it upon themselves to solve problems affecting the group as a whole the more the group will come to depend upon the leader to solve all of its problems. The reason this is more difficult an issue than that of non-participation is that the monopolizer is seen by many to be a powerful figure in the group and the confrontation between the leader and the monopolizer is often interpreted as some kind of power struggle. This is another strong reason for encouraging the group as a whole to solve its problems.

Have you heard ...? A third problem in many kinds of groups is story telling. This takes two forms. In the first form the person simply rambles through anecdotes and stories which they regard as relevant to the work of the group but which others do not – known as the 'Have I got a story for you!' problem. The second form of this difficulty is when a person seeks to 'top' a story offered by another group member – they say 'A similar thing happened to me, only more so ...' or 'Yes, but worse than that ...'. These problems need to be dealt with by the leader reminding the group of the nature of the group and its contract. If they persist then the leader might usefully suggest that the group needs some rules about language. For example, to try to talk about experiences in the 'here and now' and to use 'I–me' kinds of statements rather than 'you–them'. The language rules suggested in Chapter 7 are useful rules for groups. The real problem here is usually that the group as a whole is engaged in story-telling, hence the need to use this fact as an opportunity for teaching some language skills pertinent to self-disclosure.

We have ways of ... A fourth dificulty that sometimes arises in groups is known as the interrogation problem – it occurs when a person uses a disclosure by another to interrogate and push that person beyond what they are willing to disclose. For example, here is an extract from a group session in which Tony was interrogating Chris:

Chris: The first thing was I didn't feel that I could deal with him being so, I don't know, aggressive ...
Tony: You mean you don't know whether he was aggressive?

Chris: Well, I mean, I think he was aggressive, yes.

Tony: You think he was aggressive, but you don't sound sure. It sounds to me like the only thing you're sure of is that you felt weak whenever he was around.

Chris: Well, I did feel insecure whenever he was around but that was because he was aggressive – I don't like aggression.

Tony: Chris, it sounds to me that you like things to be neat and tidy, to be calm and constant, to be safe and secure – what are you frightened of?

Chris: You're making a lot of assumptions there ...

Tony: They are made on the evidence your current behaviour and your statements provide me with.

Chris: God, you're something, aren't you!

Tony: Are you getting upset now ... do you see me as being aggressive, Chris, am I like the person you were talking about? Chris, what are you afraid of?

This 'pushing' of one person by another can be a valuable aid to their development, but only when they consider the pushing to be undertaken from mutual respect and trust, genuineness and warmth. The tone of Tony's comments was chilled and not genuine and it was this that caused Chris to feel that Tony's questions were more like an interrogation. The leader, in this case, intervened and asked Chris to say to Tony how she felt about the way Tony was asking her these questions – to comment on the process rather than upon the content of the questions. This intervention led to a major stage of the group being concerned with genuineness and warmth and Tony seeking to explain that he was trying to help Chris see her problems as within her rather than residing in others. The quality of the group was improved by the leader drawing attention to the process the group was using to permit this interrogation. The interrogation ended and the leader thanked Tony for enabling the discussion of process to take place. This leadership intervention – calling attention to the process and providing a positive connotation to the person who was giving rise to concern – is an effective strategy for dealing with this issue.

If I were you ... A fifth problem is *advice giving.* Groups which are intended to enable a person to discover their own meaning and value and to provide them with a basis for changing the way they think and feel about themselves – a succinct description of a counselling group – provide a forum for people to offer advice and suggestions. The problem comes when such behaviour becomes a device to inhibit the individual from advising themselves and finding their own solutions to their own difficulties. There is a simple intervention the leader can use which usually resolves this difficulty. If a member wishes to offer a suggestion or advice to another person then they should ask that individual if they are willing to accept a suggestion before the suggestion is made. If the leader is concerned that the group or an individual within it is becoming over advice-oriented then a ground-rule of this kind provides an opportunity for the leader to make an intervention directed at the process of the group rather than at the content of the advice given. This is normally an effective way of dealing with the problem.

Band-aiding. A related problem – the sixth mentioned here – is known as 'band-aiding' or rescuing. What happens is this. Someone in the group is experiencing distress or difficulty or is expressing anxiety; someone else in the group rescues this person from their anxiety or distress before the person has asked for help. The result is that the person who is experiencing the anxiety or distress is rescued whether or not they wish to be. You may find it strange that some people wish to experience distress and anxiety and that they don't want to be rescued: the fact is that a great deal of personal learning and development occurs at precisely those moments when we are struggling to cope and to come to terms with distress and anxiety – personally significant learning often involves pain. By rescuing a person who is struggling to learn from their experience of distress or anxiety the rescuer is preventing that person from having the opportunity to learn more about themselves. A helpful ground-rule the leader may wish to establish if rescuing is a repeated feature of the group is to draw attention to this issue and suggest that a rescue is appropriate when, and only when, the person requests help in dealing with a problem. That is, rescues occur when someone in the group sends up a flare for themselves which says, 'Please rescue me, I am stuck'.

Hostilities break out. Linked to the problem of interrogation is the seventh problem: hostility between group members. There are occasions when a group has within it two people who become bitter enemies (most often they were bitter enemies before the group began). So bitter is their disagreement with each other that it affects the group's work and is seen to be a sign of warlike hostilities. Often the issue is dealt with by the group and the group seeks to ensure that the hostilities between these persons are kept to events that occur between group sessions or outside the group. If the group does not seek to deal with the issue then the leader needs to deal with it, either by having a private talk with the people concerned, or by confronting the issue within the group (since it affects the group as a whole) or by asking one or both of the hostile persons to leave the group. If this issue is not dealt with then the group's work will be severely impaired.

What do you think, sir? One danger of the leader's position is that the group can quickly become dependent upon the leader to the point where the group is disabled or impaired by such dependency. This problem, the eighth to be examined here, is a serious issue. It usually means that the leader has not developed a clear philosophy of groupwork and has permitted themselves to occupy the central role in the group to the exclusion of other people with resources in the group. This issue is stronger in some kinds of groups than others – for example, in a group in which it is intended that the leader teach some social skills it would be surprising if the leader did not occupy such a central position. But where it is an issue the leader ought to share the feeling that they feel they are being depended upon and renegotiate the contract, paying especial attention to the leader's role.

I think, therefore ... The final problem to be mentioned here is the intellectualizing of personal and emotional experiences. This occurs when the group is searching for universal rules, models and concepts with which to understand what is happening either within the group or for a particular person. The language rules mentioned in Chapter 7 are useful here, as are leader interventions aimed at ensuring that individuals do not seek to over-generalize their own experiences or those of others. Some of the activities suggested in Chapter 7 for work with individuals at the level of feeling – exaggeration, the empty chair, reversals – are useful in making clear the difference between intellectual statements about thoughts and feelings and the direct experience and expression of thoughts and feelings.

These are some of the problems those of you wishing to establish and maintain a counselling group are likely to experience – they are also common problems in other kinds of groups. Leaders can generally deal with these issues once they have developed a clear philosophy of groupwork for themselves.

Conclusion

If you are new to groupwork and wish to become involved, then a sensible preparation is to attend groups run by others. You will also need to develop a philosophy of groupwork that will provide you with a framework to understand and evaluate what is happening in the groups which you run. The absence of such a philosophy and previous experience of being a group member will make your work considerably more difficult than it needs to be.

One final point. Beginning group leaders often feel more responsible for the experience of group members than they should. Group members are able to take responsibility for their own actions and for their own well-being and do not need to be rescued from their own self-thoughts unless they specifically ask for your help. Ensure that group members know that they can ask for your help, but do not thrust it upon them because of your concern to make sure that everyone has a good group experience. Allow the members of your group to be themselves.

Suggested reading

Corey, G. and Corey, M.S. (1977) *Groups – Processes and Practice*. Monterey, Ca: Brooks Cole.
An elegant, thorough and vivid introduction to groupwork of various kinds. What some readers might find over-simplistic is in fact a very succinct account of groupwork as experienced by both participants and leaders. Highly recommended.

Rogers, C.R. (1979) *On Encounter Groups*. Harmondsworth: Penguin Books.
A slim but thorough introduction to the philosophy, practice and experience of encounter groups written with sensitivity and a great deal of insight. Invaluable source of understanding the dynamics of groups.

Douglas, Tom (1968) *Groupwork*. London: Tavistock.
This is a standard text for social workers in training, and as such is very valuable. The author takes a particular stance about groups and explores their utility within this framework. Rather a difficult read for someone without a sociology/psychology or social work background.

Jacobs, A. and Spradlin, W. (eds) (1974) *The Group as an Agent of Change*. New York: Behavioural Publications.
A detailed and thorough set of readings which looks at the value of groups in a variety of settings – family, mental hospital and mental health programme, school, community organization and church. Many of the ideas and descriptions documented here could be applied to almost any group setting. A useful compendium.

Chapter 11

Helping through Networks

As a helper or counsellor you are not alone. Others are engaged in the same task, whether through acquaintance with a person in need, through other professional roles or through some other organization. This chapter is concerned with ways of connecting the person you are helping to their own networks of social support and with the ways in which you can connect yourself to helping networks.

It is worth noting that a great deal of available research suggests that being connected to social support networks acts as an effective buffer to stress and anxiety. For example, in the work of Leonard Pearlin and Carmi Schooler, described more fully in Chapter 4, it was shown that those who actively associated with others through a personal support network (for example, family, relatives, friends and work-mates) experienced certain events as less stressful than those who did not feel connected in this way. Feeling socially supported enables concerns, doubts and worries to be shared in such a way as to reduce their stress-bearing potential.

Networks operate all the time and take a variety of forms. For example, information about jobs most often comes from people who are in work sharing information about new openings or retirements in their own place of work. Parent networks are constantly exchanging goods (clothes, equipment and toys) that are no longer needed by one family but which are thought to be useful by another. Women have grouped themselves together to resource themselves and study women's health problems and have started a network of Well Women Clinics. When a person is experiencing a loss – bereavement or the loss of a job, for example – family members, friends and relatives frequently create a network to help them cope emotionally and materially with their new status. A final example: most teenagers find out about sex and sexuality from their friends rather than from their parents or from school – the peer network is effective in providing information and advice for this age-group. All these are examples of networks in action.

Most of the networks people use are *informal* – they involve friendships that evolve over time, relationships that are inevitable given the person's work or family position, or contacts the person makes through the interests that they have. But not all networks are informal; some are specifically created to provide a basis for people to make contact with each other, to share ideas and experiences and to give support to one another. For example, the Well Women Clinics mentioned earlier are examples of a deliberate attempt to network ideas and resources from one community to another; there are networks devoted to helping widows, depressives and the unemployed; there are networks aimed at the promotion of learning; and networks devoted to personal growth and development. Networks can be created which serve a variety of functions and purposes. What I am concerned with here is understanding those networks which are most useful to the person in need and to yourself.

Networks and the person in need

When a person seeks help from a stranger it is often a sign that their own helping networks are inadequate. It may be that the person is disconnected from their own networks – family, friends or relatives – or that they have never been that connected to such a network. It may be that they are connected to this network, but its resources are inadequate given the problem the person is experiencing. How can you help this person connect with and stay involved with a network?

The first thing you need to do is to understand the value of a supportive network for a person in need. Networks can serve six functions:

- providing a basis for the person to feel and be attached and associated with others
- providing a basis for a person to integrate with a community or group in such a way as to help that person recognize and live with social norms
- providing the person with a source of nourishment and support for their ideas and their development
- ensuring that the person is able to use others for the purpose of guidance, advice giving and information
- providing some stability and reliability in relationships – 'If all

else fails, I can always turn to my friends'
- networks value individuals who are a part of them – thus networks can be said to offer the person a reassurance of their own worth.

These functions of networks are not automatically met simply by being involved with others – they concern the quality of relationships rather than just the fact that people can and do meet with each other. The individual needs to feel that these things either happen or are possible if they are to use a network in a supportive and helping way.

Given such a potential for a network, the helper needs to establish the extent to which the person is connected to a network of friends, relatives and family members and the extent to which the person feels that this network is serving these kinds of purposes. There are several questions that the helper can usefully ask to establish the size and nature of the network used by the person in need. Some of these questions are listed here:

- Who would care for their home or car if they were out of town for a while?
- If they are in work, who at work do they talk to most often about work-related matters?
- Who, if anyone, has helped with household tasks in the last three months?
- Who do they see as their social friends – people they would go for a drink with or to a movie?
- With whom do they talk about their hobbies or interests?
- If unmarried, who is their 'best' friend?
- With whom do they talk about their personal worries?
- Whose advice do they consider in making important decisions?
- From whom (if they could) would they borrow a large sum of money?
- Who are the adults who live in the same house?

By asking these questions and exploring the answers that are given, the helper is able to build a picture of the person's helping and support network. There are other questions that might be relevant, especially those about the quality of the person's contact:

- How many people do you know who could come to see you at any time and wouldn't mind if the house was untidy or if you were in the middle of a meal?
- Are there any people you can lean on in times of difficulty whom

you know you can rely upon to give real help – personal help, not just practical assistance?
- Is there any one person without whom life would be just intolerable?
- When you are worried, or in a difficult situation, is there any one person you go to for advice or guidance?
- Is there anyone who tells you or makes you feel that you are good at the things you do at home or at work or with others?
- Which of the people you have mentioned know each other?

These two sets of questions tell us about the size of the person's support network and its quality. They also help us identify the extent to which the person is connected or disengaged from others. In addition, the second set of questions helps us to examine the way in which individuals in the network are connected to each other.

The value of exploring these questions is that it enables the helper to develop a map of the person's active support network – I often physically draw a map to make sure I have understood the information I have gained correctly and I check out my drawing with the person in need. In addition, the questions highlight the extent to which this person is currently using their network and the way in which they see themselves in relation to it. Often it is helpful to explain the value of a network to them – the six points mentioned earlier become strong points to be explored with the person. It is sometimes necessary to examine how the way in which the person uses their network is a part of their problem, since often a person in need ceases to be effective in their contact with others (see also Chapter 4).

Do not be fooled by the fact that a person has a large number of contacts. *Size* of the network is not the same as network *quality*. A person who is surrounded by friends and helpers may not be getting the same kind of support as a person who has one or two 'very close' friends. Also, a person with a very close relationship with their spouse may not have such a supportive network as a person who has a good relationship with his or her spouse and a close relationship with someone else. Seek to understand the person's support network in terms of its quality across the kinds of issues listed in the second set of questions.

Some of those that the person in need lists as helpful may well be professional helpers – social workers or social service employees, teachers, nurses, doctors. I have found it useful to draw a map of the network of support the person has in terms of three 'layers'. *Layer one* is the person's closest friends and supporters – his or her primary network; *layer two* is the network of informal helpers associated with some club, group or organization to which the person belongs – church groups, clubs, womens groups; the *final layer* is the layer of people who are paid as helpers and supporters of persons in need – the formal network. Figure 2 shows this 'model' of a network. I sometimes use it (or a specially made-up version with the names of friends, relatives, workmates and informal helpers listed) as a basis for discussing the person's care network. This tends to trigger more detailed responses to questions about the quality of that network whilst at the same time helping me locate my own role amidst that of others.

The aim of exploring someone's network is to connect them better to it. Often this can best be done by:

• encouraging them to see the network as being capable of more than they have hitherto used it for – the six points earlier are useful here

• suggesting better questions to ask of network members – in essence, teaching some social skills associated with effective use of networks

• showing them and rehearsing with them the possible uses of the network, perhaps by role-play or guided exploration.

In the end the focus is often upon returning them to seeing the primary layer as the most useful and frequent source of help that they are able to use. A related aim is therefore to reduce their dependence upon the formal network and increase their use of the informal and primary networks.

One final point in this section. A person in need may be a member of a family and may feel that the family is a useful source of guidance and information about some things, but is unable to help with the specific concerns they now have. This often arises with teenagers experiencing some difficulty in personal relationships or with older people facing up to major decisions which they do not wish their children to be disturbed by. The helper may need to act as a surrogate family member in many ways on such occasions. But it is important that the helper ensures that the person in need continues to recognize the value of their family for other needs and that the helper sees their intervention as short-term, time-limited and specific. A failure to caution an intervention in this way can create further problems for the person in need and cast the helper in the role of problem-maker rather than problem-solver. The need for a specific contract here is clear, especially when the person in need

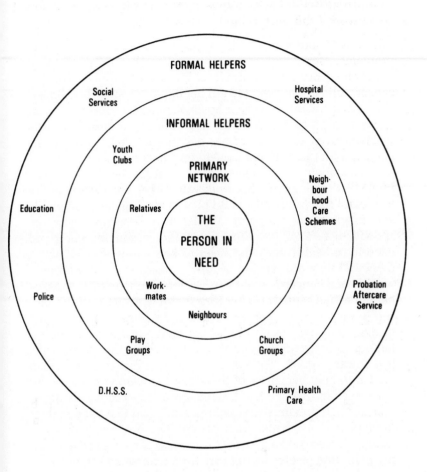

Figure 2.

makes it clear that they do not want their family involved in something which they inevitably will be involved in at a later stage.

To illustrate the situation just described, here is a brief description
of some work I did with Julia.

> Julia was 76 and very ill with a cancer of the lung and cardiac
> problems. Her daughter and son-in-law (her only relatives)
> knew about her cardiac problems but did not know about her
> cancer. Julia did not want to tell her daughter about her illness.
> Nor did she want to receive hospital treatment for her illness
> – she wanted to die at home as painlessly as possible. Julia
> received poor advice from her doctor, so I helped her make
> contact with the National Society for Cancer Relief and helped
> her think about the implications of what she was doing. Most
> important throughout this time was to get her to realize the
> important role her family could play in making her comfortable
> and in giving her support. Whilst they need not know the
> specific nature of her illness and the reason for her rapid
> decline in health, they did need to know how she felt about
> them and they did need to be able to share some of their own
> worries and concerns about her. I contracted with Julia to assist
> her to receive support for her illness and to act as a trusted per-
> son – almost like a nephew who 'knew how to handle such
> things' (this was her phrase for my role) – in exchange for her
> talking to her daugher and son-in-law about the feelings she
> had towards them. Though she died five months after I had
> started to help her, three of these months were very happy for
> her – she felt that she had become even closer to her daughter
> than she had previously thought possible and that her daughter
> 'understood' her better than before. The last two months of
> Julia's life were taken up with the process of dying and alleviat-
> ing pain. She received daily care from a nurse and from a doc-
> tor and her daughter 'lived in' during this time. My contract
> changed – the doctor told the daughter why her mother was
> dying and my contract became one of spending some time each
> week with both of them simply helping them experience the
> grief that they felt. I also ensured that the daughter was able to
> talk to her husband about her feelings through a regular session
> with them.

In this example, the role I played was one of networker within
agreed limits and within a family network. In other cases – for example, with a pregnant 15-year-old who did not want her parents to

know that she was to have a baby – the role of the helper is more difficult to define and the nature of the role will change as the person in need comes to view their situation differently.

Networks and the helper

The model of a helping network stresses that you as a helper are not alone, whatever layer of the network you are associated with. To be effective as a helper you should know about the other resources available to the person in need and the resources which you could refer that person to. That is, you need to be connected to the network of helpers and their skills.

This involves finding out about:

- The range of services available in your area or within reasonable travelling distances. That is, the kinds of organizations, the nature of the case loads which these organizations work with, and the quality of the services provided by different agencies.
- Who is available within each of these agencies – it is better to get to know a named person within an organization well than just to know the name and phone number of the organization.
- What links the individuals within each of the organizations have to others – don't see an individual as an end point, see them as the beginning of a way in to other connections and as a way of extending your own network.
- How you can collaborate with these other persons without the collaboration meaning that you change your work in a way that you do not wish.

These points strongly suggest that you need to get to know other helpers as people rather than as professionals or organizational representatives; you need to get to know how they think about the people they help and what kind of work they do well; you need to recognize the value others have for helping you solve your problems and to see others as a way of strengthening your work rather than as sources of interference or disruption. Most critically, you need to know who will accept your judgement about the people you are helping, so that when you wish them to help you they will be willing to do so.

These suggestions for your own networking activity are difficult to implement, especially if you lead a busy life or live in a rural community. But the effort is worth it. Knowing the people in the helping network in this way will enable you to:

- refer those in need to appropriate sources of advice and guidance
- obtain advice that will help you help others
- ensure that you see your work in the context of the range of helping services available in the community in which you are placed.

Three words of advice about developing such a network of contacts for your own use. First, don't be territorial – see your work as part of a greater movement of activity. Just because you like to work with marital problems does not mean that you are the only person who should do so: recognize that your efforts are always a part of a network of helping efforts. Second, don't put boundaries on the people in your helper's network – just because a person works in an agency devoted to helping individuals deal with drinking problems does not mean that this is all that person can help with – recognize their interests and skills as having general qualities. Finally, the best way to get to know others in the helper network is to collaborate, co-operate or work with them in some way. This may be on specific projects, or at a workshop or during some training event. But doing something with someone is a good basis for getting to know about them as individuals.

Conclusion

The helper needs to recognize that their own work is generally relative and a part of a larger canvas of helping within the community. The less connected the helper is to local networks the more likely it is that the person in need is being restricted by the helper's own ignorance of available services. In my own case, for example, I rarely undertake any sex therapy since there is an excellent service available locally – the same is true of work on bereavement and on social skills. Were I not to be connected, my own helping skills and resources would be stretched over such a wide territory of work that I would not feel confident that those I was helping were getting the best possible service. The question I therefore ask myself when someone seeks my help is: 'Am I the best person to help this individual right now, and if not who do I know who could effectively help them?'. This is not to say that the person seeking my help is always willing to be referred to someone else, but if I really feel that I am not best able to help I will say no, seek to encourage and enable a referral and not act as a helper for that person.

Being associated with a network of helpers through informal contact is a significant way of creating self-support opportunities for the helper. Others with helping roles provide suggestions, advice, information, guidance and contacts which continually enrich the work that a helper does. Being disconnected from such a network means that the helper is losing opportunities to be involved and associated with others and is losing an opportunity for enrichment. The message, then, is 'connect for health'; after all, this is the advice we are essentially giving those we are seeking to help.

One final point. The helper has a responsibility which goes beyond that which he or she has towards the person in need. Sometimes private troubles are indicative of public issues. The helper will occasionally have to make a decision about the extent to which they should make known to others in their community the way in which particular phenomena – unemployment, abuse in families, the effects of divorce on children, or alcoholism all come to mind as examples – affect the psychological and social well-being of their community. They may also have to comment on the way in which they and others (social workers, policemen, lawyers, doctors, etc.) are responding to the phenomena. Helpers have a responsibility to bring to the attention of the community in which they are placed issues which arise out of their work. Be careful. There are ethical (see Chapter 3) and political issues at stake when such disclosures are made. Do it carefully – through a group, an association – rather than sensationally. Make sure that the message is getting to those people who could act. Protect the individuals involved. But do not shrink from the implications of your work with those in need for the social institutions designed to serve them.

Suggested reading

Heller, K. and Monahan, J. (1977) *Psychology and Community Change.* Chicago: The Dorsey Press.
A psychologist's introduction to community development and networking which contains many useful examples of community activity involving psychological and social work practices. Not an easy read, but invaluable for those who are experienced community development workers seeking to increase their academic knowledge.

Welch, M.S. (1980) *Networking – The Great New Way for Women to Get Ahead.* New York: Harcourt Brace Jovanovich.
A practical guide to the way in which women have organized themselves so as to facilitate personal development and increased resources for women.

Practical Exercises

These exercises and activities are intended to help you practise and develop some of the skills outlined in this book. You should use and adapt them to suit your circumstances. They are intended for use with friends and colleagues.

Exercise 1: Feelings. Write down on small pieces of paper as many adjectives describing as many different feeling states as possible (e.g., guilty, depressed, sad, joyous, happy, amused, bored, wishful). In turn, each person picks out one of these pieces of paper from a hat and silently portrays the feeling state. Others have to guess which state is being displayed. Notice how many different reactions there are and how difficult it is to discriminate accurately between certain feelings. The more pieces of paper and the fewer people the better.

Exercise 2: Social Support. Using the questions given in the final chapter (see pages 152–153), construct a social support 'map' for yourself and a few friends. Use this as a basis for talking with these friends about the value of social support to them. Does having such a network reduce stress? What key things is it about social support that make a difference? How would they encourage others to improve the quality of their social support network?

Exercise 3: Contracting. Find a partner who is willing to discuss recent happenings in their life. Offer a contract to help them by listening. Use the contract types listed on page 125. Listen. Then reverse roles, with you negotiating a contract for yourself. Notice how difficult sticking to the contract can be – notice what difference it makes when you do.

Exercise 4: Thinking. On pages 74–75 a number of irrational beliefs are listed. Write each of these out on small cards. Give the cards to friends and ask them to react to the item on each card by telling you something about themselves where they can recognise this (or a very similar belief) being the basis for their behaviour. Whilst listening, see if you can articulate the ideas of Chapter 6 and see if you can add to this list of irrational beliefs.

Exercise 5: Groupwork. Imagine you are going to run a group on a particular theme – say stress or problem solving. Write out the 'further particulars' for this group. What would you need to say? What information would they need? What ethical statements would need to be made?

Exercise 6: Feelings. For each of the following phrases identify others which mean almost the same. Then make notes about the differences between your phrases and the ones given here.

- 'I'm not sure whether anyone really likes me or whether I am the kind of person that no one likes to know.'
- 'I hate being forced to be angry whenever I'm pushed around.'
- 'All I really want is for people to accept me.'
- 'I just get depressed whenever things turn out the way I thought they would.'
- 'One day things will get better, but right now that day looks so far away that I'm not sure I'll make it.'

Give this same list of phrases to a friend and get them to draw up their own list of 'nearly the sames' and compare them.

Exercise 7: Group Leadership. After leading some kind of group (see Chapter 10), assess yourself on a scale of 0–100 (with 60 being satisfactory) on each of the following statements.

- 'I was authentic and true to myself throughout that group.'
- 'I was clear about the aims and purposes of the group at all times.'
- 'I communicated my trust and respect for other people.'
- 'I showed that I was receptive to the needs, ideas and reactions of others.'
- 'I faced up to facts and reactions honestly.'
- 'I encouraged and assisted others when they wished to participate.'
- 'I was able to provide space for people to enjoy what they did today.'

Using this list and your self-ratings, outline a series of steps you feel you need to take to develop groupwork skills.

Exercise 8: Burn-out. This is *not* an easy task! For one week contract with yourself to keep a diary of both the positive and negative feelings you have about your helping activities. Do not enter details of situations (e.g., 'didn't like the fact that so-and-so goes on about his mother's influence, and won't accept that he's permitted himself to be so influenced'). Instead, enter your reactions to situations (e.g., 'I notice that I sometimes get irritated when the person in need doesn't have the same insights as I do'). At the end of the week, review your diary with a colleague or a friend and identify some learning tasks for yourself. Also, count the number of times certain things come up and look at the balance between positive and negative – then re-read Chapter 9.

Conclusion
These are just a few exercises. You can find more in the following books:

Brandes, D. and Phillips, H. (1979) *Gamester's Handbook.* London: Hutchinson.
Brandes, D. (1982) *Gamester's Handbook Two.* London: Hutchinson.
Egan, G. (1982) *Exercises in Helping Skills.* Monterey, Ca: Brooks Cole.

If you would like some improvisation activities which have relevance to counselling and helping and are also fun, then K. Johnstone's *IMPRO – Improvisation and the Theatre* (London: Methuen, 1981) contains many ideas which you can use directly or with variations. Whilst all the exercises listed here have a serious purpose, they do not have to be conducted in a sombre way.

Index